THE BIRDS

ARISTOPHANES

THE BIRDS

Translated into English verse with

Introduction and Notes

by

GILBERT MURRAY

O.M., D.C.L.

Formerly Regius Professor of Greek
in the
University of Oxford

OXFORD UNIVERSITY PRESS

NEW YORK

1950

INTRODUCTION

The Birds is not perhaps the funniest of Aristophanes'
plays, but it is by general agreement the most delightful.
It has not the fire of the *Knights* or the *Wasps*, nor the
curiously modern issues of thought that startle us in
the *Clouds* and the *Frogs*. For once the stormy dramatist
has allowed himself a play of escape, escape by means
of imagination into a care-free world, far away from
the great war-wearied city, with its taxes and regulations
and prohibitions and fines and the follies of its exasper-
ated *demos;* away from mankind, creatures "so dimly
alive," shadows and pursuers of shadows, toiling so
much and accomplishing so little; away perhaps even
from the gods who now claim to rule the world, and
are making such a very poor business of it. There is a
tradition, he might remember, that our ancestors had
other gods before these anthropomorphic Olympians
were introduced; sometimes, it may be, they worshipped birds; how much more sensible! The Birds
ask for so little, and have so much to give. They want
no great temples or sacrifices; they insist on no long
pilgrimages before they will speak to us. They are
here, living, flying and singing among us; we can see
the joy that is in their hearts, joy that we creatures
of clay can never reach. Yet if we worshipped them
rightly, who knows?, they might let us have some
share in it.

Aristophanes must have known his birds very well;

he names an extraordinary number of species, some of which even Professor Darcy Thompson has not been able to identify. Of course he makes them all ridiculous, except perhaps the Nightingale; he laughs at them and loves them, and he seems to have, almost alone in antiquity, a Blake-like hatred of seeing a bird caged or tethered.

Life in Athens must have been difficult in 414 B.C., when this play was produced, a year of wild hope and anxiety and suspicion. The previous year had seen the unprovoked siege and massacre of Melos, which seems to have been selected by Thucydides for detailed analysis as forming the climax of the ever-growing violence characteristic of the dominant ultra-democratic war-party, and must have cast a gloom on the more conscientious minority who were now powerless. It was immediately followed by an expedition, with the greatest naval force ever seen, to establish the Athenian rule over Syracuse and all Sicily and perhaps more. Was this a splendid military enterprise, or was it, as the old poets would have said, a manifest case of *Hubris* begetting *Atê* and leading to certain death? Opinion was divided; the brilliant and ambitious Alcibiades was for the adventure, the experienced and hitherto successful Nikias against it. Just before the fleet sailed, however, there occurred a curious outrage which shows how closely enlightened Athens was still haunted by primitive superstitious fears. The stone pillars with human heads and symbols of fertility, called "Hermae," which stood as landmarks through-

6

out the city, were, all but one, mutilated in a single night. Later inquiries led to the conclusion that it was only a drunken frolic by members of a smart and "enlightened" oligarchic club, but to the mass of the people such a mutilation was an omen of the worst possible significance. Coming to an overstrained populace on the very eve of their greatest and most dangerous enterprise, it produced a storm of hysterical alarm and suspicion. There were rumours of malignant treason; rumours of profanations of the mysteries. Informers, oracle-mongers, political charlatans, all the classes whom Aristophanes most detested, set to work to stir up trouble and persecution. And, though no disaster to the Sicilian armada had yet occurred, to men like Aristophanes the atmosphere must have been such as to intensify the worry and discontent produced by the long war and the concentration of power in the hands of men whom they despised. He did not protest as he had in the *Knights, Acharnians* and *Wasps*. Perhaps it was too dangerous after the law passed in 415 forbidding personal attacks in comedy. Perhaps he was merely anxious not to increase the existing trouble and discord. He took refuge in poetry. He makes passing allusions to a great many artists and public men in the course of the play, so many that I have thought it helpful to make an alphabetical list of them. He lashes a few of his old *bêtes noires* like the fat warmonger Cleônymus; but on the whole he keeps clear of politics, and entirely clear of the most dangerous issues. There is no mention of the Hermae or the

Sicilian expedition. No doubt he had his prejudices, but it is worth noting that nearly all the individuals whom he pillories in *The Birds* are condemned by subsequent history.

The last few scenes of the play are exceedingly funny, but it seems odd that, at a time of so much religious excitement in Athens, they did not lead to a prosecution for impiety. The gods are deposed. The sceptre is restored to the Birds; Pithetaerus takes to wife a mysterious "Basileia," or Queen, and thereupon is accepted as King of the world in place of Zeus, with special control over rain, thunder and lightning. This seems to us like flat blasphemy. To the Greeks, however, the idea of a god-King being superseded by a new god-King was a familiar feature in the ordinary Vegetation or New Year celebrations. Zeus as a Year God would naturally be succeeded by a New Zeus; indeed the name Dionysus itself is generally interpreted as "Zeus-Young" or "Zeus-Son." And there was one particular Athenian festival which seems to agree very aptly with the last scene of *The Birds.* On the eve of the twelfth day of the Anthesteria the god Dionysus was ritually married to the "Basilinna," or "Little Queen." The Queen's part was played by the wife of the Archon Basileus, who went by night to meet her bridegroom escorted by a rout of "Hours, Nymphs and Maenads": that of Dionysus, by a "very old wooden image" of the god, which was apparently a rather grotesque object and never exhibited to public view except on this one annual occasion. The termination—*inna*, as in Corinna (*Mädchen*), and Erinna or Herinna (*Little Hera*), turns Basileia into a pet name or diminutive. Though the details of the Sacred Marriage were "not to be spoken," and the advocate *Against Neaira* (Demosthenes 49) professes suitable horror at his opponent's breach of its ritual, there seems to have been an air of gaiety about this union of the "Little Queen" and the "Young Zeus," which is borne out by some of the representations of the rite on Attic vases. Such ceremonies have always a religious or mystical side, but there is also, as in our own Christmas, a festive side, which often preponderates. The result of the marriage, it would seem, was to establish Dionysus as the New King. We read, for example, in the Orphica (fr. 190): "His father seats him on the royal throne, puts the sceptre in his hand, and makes him king of the Cosmic gods," especially giving him power over lightning and thunder. Thus Pithetaerus in his marriage with "The Queen" seems exactly to fill the rôle of Dionysus.

It is always extremely difficult to understand, in an alien religion, where liberties may be taken and where the slightest liberty is an offence. The medieval mystery plays supply many examples. In Athens it is worth remembering what a gulf there seems to have been between the true objects of local worship, on which the life of the earth depended, and the mere Homeric Olympians, with their roots not in the soil but in the myths of the poets. Iris and Zeus, and of course the newcomer Dionysus, were fair game for comedy; but the Hermae were a serious matter and no one would take risks with Athena, the native Korê.

This thought leads to another, which takes us into unexplored and perhaps unexplorable regions of Greek religious history. The chief claim made in Pithetaerus's preposterous speech to the Birds is, after all, partly true. The Birds were objects of worship to the Minoans and the early inhabitants of Greece before Zeus and his Olympian commando descended upon the peninsula. Birds were not gods; Pithetaerus does not quite say they were. Yet the bird perched on the sacred Double Axe or the pillar-tree was the *Numen* of the axe or the tree. The Minoans believed, as Nilson says, that the gods—or, to put it more exactly, the divine power— appeared in the form of birds. Again, the most important and wide-spread method of communication with the divine power was by augury. The birds knew the weather; they knew when good luck or bad was to be expected; they gave clear warning of the future to those who could read their messages. Could they have known what was coming so well unless indeed it was partly they who made it come? After the invasion of the Olympians particular birds are found as "attributes" of the various gods, but in the opinion of most students of the subject the "attribute" was there before its possessor.

To us these thoughts are speculations of the learned; what were they to Aristophanes? Not conscious speculations of course. He did not explicitly reflect that Athena was the true *Athênaia Korê* and not merely a War-goddess sprung from the brain of Olympian Zeus; but he seems to have felt the difference. He was also familiar with augury. He knew many stories of gods in bird form; he knew there was some meaning in the birds perched on the sceptres or the heads of kings; had he ever seen any remnants of the birds on the Minoan pillars? We do not know. I suspect that these subjects of our recondite learning, in a looser and less thought-out form, were to him things so familiar as not to need talking about.

Poetry is a highly perishable article. Humour more perishable still. The sentiment at which our grandparents wept is apt to leave us cold. The topical allusion which was a hit last year is mostly a miss now. Elizabethan clowns are more often tedious than funny. Yet the fun of Aristophanes somehow survives, and so does the poetry. It needs, no doubt, a certain effort, an effort of historical imagination and sympathy, to enjoy a comedy full of so topical allusions, so characteristic of its time and birthplace, as *The Birds;* but it is beyond doubt a thing of beauty, and it rests with us to keep it a joy for ever.

CHARACTERS IN THE PLAY

PITHETAERUS, an elderly Athenian gentleman.

EUELPIDES, his companion.

TÊREUS, formerly King of Thrace, now transformed into a HOOPOE.

TROCHILUS, Servant to Têreus.

A PRIEST.

A POET.

A PROPHET.

METON, the astronomer.

A COMMISSAR.

A LAW-MONGER.

IRIS, the Goddess.

A HERALD.

A FATHER-BEATER.

KINÊSIAS, the Lyric Poet.

AN INFORMER.

PROMÊTHEUS.

POSEIDON.

HÊRACLES.

A TRIBALLIAN.

MESSENGERS, SERVANTS, ETC.

CHORUS OF BIRDS.

"The play was produced in the Archonship of Chabrias (414 B.C.) in the name of Callistratus and obtained the Second Prize. First, Ameipsias with *The Revellers*; third, Phrynichus with *The Solitary*." THE ANCIENT ARGUMENT.

THE BIRDS

*The scene at the back represents a great rock in a wood.
Enter two Travellers; the first, an elderly man of
commanding presence, is led by a Crow on a string, the
second, plump and cheerful, similarly led by a Jackdaw.
Their names are not known till, at l. 645, the First
Traveller announces himself as PITHETAERUS, a
fictitious name meaning "Companion-Persuader" or
"Born Leader," and his companion as EUELPIDES,
"Hopefulson."*

EUELPIDES   [*To his Jackdaw.*

Straight on, you say? On to the tree up there?

PITHETAERUS

Confound the creature! Mine is croaking "Back."

EUELPIDES

But why do we do it? Trapesing up and down,
Backward and forward, like two shuttlecocks,
With no sense? It'll be the death of us.

PITHETAERUS

To think I should have tramped a hundred miles
And more, by orders of a wretched crow!

15

EUELPIDES

And I, by orders of a cruel jackdaw,
Have stubbed my toe-nails off. Just think of it!

PITHETAERUS

I don't know where on earth we are by now.
Could you ever find your fatherland again?

EUELPIDES

From this place? No; who could? Not even that man
Who has so many, Exekestides.
Oh Hell!

PITHETAERUS

Is that yours? Go there if you like.

EUELPIDES   [*To the Audience.*

He swindled us, that man from Orneai,
The crack-brained poulterer, Philocrates.
He said this pair would lead us to the Hoopoe,
Tereus, the man who changed into a bird.
He sold us for one obol this young son
Of impudence, and that old dame for three;
But the only thing they knew was how to bite.

[*To the Jackdaw.*

Hallo, you're gaping, are you? What's that for?
You want to lead us further through the rocks?
There's no road this way.

THE BIRDS

PITHETAERUS

Not a vestige here
Of any track.

Your crow is saying something
About the road.

PITHETAERUS

She's croaking, but it's not
The same croak as it was.

EUELPIDES

What does she say
About the road?

PITHETAERUS

The road?—She only says
She means to peck my toes off and then eat them.

EUELPIDES   [*To the Audience.*

Now really, gentlemen, I put it to you;
Isn't it hard? When we complain, they say
"Go to the crows!" We are doing our best to go there;
We're all packed up, and now can't find the way!
We're just like Sakas, the reverse way round.
He's an outsider forcing his way in;
While we, born citizens of Athens, we,

17

With every register of birth and race,
And no one scaring us, are keen to fly
From land and home—just spread our legs and fly!
Not that we dislike Athens, or pretend
She's not a very great and golden City,
And free for all men to pay taxes in.
The sweet cicada sits upon his twig
Just for a little season, warbling summer;
But the Athenians, bless them, all their lives
Sit in the law courts, warbling summonses.
That's why we are starting upon this long walk.
A pot, a basket and some myrtle sprays
Make all our luggage, and we're wandering round
To find some region not beset by worries,
Where we can set our house up and survive.
Our present journey is to see King Tereus,
The hoopoe, to enquire if he has seen
In all his world-wide flights a place like that.

PITHETAERUS

I say!

EUELPIDES

What is it?

PITHETAERUS

All this time my crow
Is signalling "up."

18

EUELPIDES

Up? So is this jackdaw;
Wide-beaked. I think he wants to show me something.
There must be birds here. . . . It's the place! Let's make
A noise and we shall soon know.

PITHETAERUS

Kick the rock!

EUELPIDES

You butt it with your head. That makes more noise.

PITHETAERUS

Well, take a stone and knock.

EUELPIDES

Yes, if you like.

[*Knocking.*

Hi, boy!

PITHETAERUS

You mustn't call the hoopoe Boy.
Say Hoopahoy, not boy.

EUELPIDES

Hi, Hoopahoy!
How long'll you keep me knocking? Hoopahoy!
[*A door opens in the rock, and out comes an enormous
bird with a formidable beak,* TROCHILUS.

TROCHILUS

What have we here? Who is it called the Master?

> [*Mutual terror between the bird and the two Travellers, during which the crow and jackdaw escape.*

EUELPIDES

Apollo, Averter of Evil, what a yawn!

TROCHILUS

God help me! Humans! It's a pair of fowlers!

EUELPIDES

No, no! Don't mention such a horrid thought!

TROCHILUS

We'll have you hanged!

EUELPIDES

Please, we are not men at all.

TROCHILUS

What are you then?

EUELPIDES

Well, I'm a Libyan bird
Called the Blue Funk.

THE BIRDS

TROCHILUS

Rubbish! And what's your friend?

PITHETAERUS

An Oriental bird called Wobble-Knees.

EUELPIDES   [*recovering himself*

But what the devil are you, what fish or fowl?

TROCHILUS

I'm just a slave bird.

EUELPIDES

Beaten by some cock

In battle?

TROCHILUS

No, but when His Majesty
Became a bird, he prayed the gods that I
Might be one too—he needed a bird's bird
To attend him.

EUELPIDES

Bless me, does a bird want servants?

TROCHILUS

He does. It's natural, having been a man.
He wants some anchovies, maybe, from Phalêron,
I take a plate and run for anchovies.
He wants some soup; we need a bowl and spoon,
I run for a bowl.

EUELPIDES

    A runner duck, by Zeus!
Well, runner, do you know what you must do?
Call out your Master to us.

TROCHILUS

    Oh, I can't.
He sleeps in the afternoon. He had a lunch
Of myrtle berries and a few white ants.

EUELPIDES

Well, wake him all the same.

TROCHILUS

    He won't be pleased,
I know he won't. Still, to oblige you two . . . [*Exit.*

PITHETAERUS

Plague take you! You half killed me with pure fright.

22

EUELPIDES

Confound it! And my jackdaw's run away
In terror.

PITHETAERUS

What a timid beast you are!
You've gone and lost your jackdaw.

EUELPIDES

I like that!
Didn't you lose your crow when you fell down?

PITHETAERUS

Lose him? Not I.

EUELPIDES

What then?

PITHETAERUS

He flew away.

HOOPOE   [*Off.*

Ho, there! I am coming out. Set wide the wood.

[*The door in the Rock opens. Enter TEREUS,
the Hoopoe.*

23

EUELPIDES

Lord Heracles, what creature have we here?
What feathering's this? What crest on crest on crest?

HOOPOE

Who is it wished to see me?

EUELPIDES

The twelve Gods,
God bless us, seem to have rather dressed you down.

HOOPOE

Sir, are you mocking? Laughing at the way
My feathers are made up? I, gentlemen,
Was once a man.

EUELPIDES

We didn't laugh at you, Sir.

HOOPOE

At what, then?

PITHETAERUS

Well, your beak looked rather funny.

HOOPOE

I'm the correct Tereus of Sophocles,
It's just like this he treats me in his plays.

24

THE BIRDS

EUELPIDES

You're Tereus? . . . Common fowl or blazing peacock?

HOOPOE [*Coldly.*

I am a bird.

EUELPIDES

What's happened to your feathers?

HOOPOE

They're moulted off.

EUELPIDES

The effect of some disease?

HOOPOE

Disease? No. Birds all moult their feathers off
In winter, and then grow another set.
But tell me, what are you two?

EUELPIDES

We? Just men.

HOOPOE

From what land?

EUELPIDES

From the Mistress of the Seas.

25

HOOPOE

Professional jurors?

EUELPIDES

Just the opposite.
Non-jurors.

HOOPOE

Does that plant grow there at all?

EUELPIDES

A little of the wild sort, if you search.

HOOPOE

And what particular purpose brings you here?

EUELPIDES

We wanted to consult you.

HOOPOE

What about?

EUELPIDES

Well, first, you once were human, so are we;
You once had debts in plenty, so have we;
You didn't much like paying, nor do we.
And then—then you were turned into a bird,
And flew round all the lands and all the seas;
And all the wisdom of both birds and men

26

Is now yours. That is why we have come to you
As suppliants, in the hope that you can show us
Some city of peace and comfort, like a rug
To lie down and curl up in, with no prickles.

HOOPOE

You want a greater city than your own?

EUELPIDES

Not greater, but more suited to our taste.

HOOPOE (*suspiciously*)
Pining for aristocracy?

EUELPIDES

                    Why, no,
The name of Skelias' son makes me feel sick.

HOOPOE

Tell me, what sort of place would please you best?

EUELPIDES

One with no public troubles worse than this:
Say a friend knocked some morning at your door,
And cried: "Beseech you, by Olympian Zeus,
Come to my house, you and your children, early
And smart. I am going to give a marriage feast.
Ah, don't desert me now! Or, if you do,
Never come near me when my luck's gone wrong."

27

HOOPOE

Bless me! You *are* in love with difficulties.
And you agree?

PITHETAERUS

I do.

HOOPOE

Well, let me see.
There is a city of the sort you want,
A pleasure city, down upon the coast
Of the Erythraean sea.

EUELPIDES

Beside the sea?
Never! Where any day the official galley
May pop up with a summons or a writ.
Couldn't you tell us of some town in Greece?

[*Pithetaerus withdraws from the conversation,
thinking.*

HOOPOE

There's Lepreon in Elis; why not go
And settle there?

EUELPIDES

Why not? I'd hate the place.
The other lepers might be like Melanthius.

28

THE BIRDS

HOOPOE

Well, there's an inland tribe, the Opuntii
In Locris.

EUELPIDES

    Not for a gold talent! No,
I won't be one of the Opuntii.
There's one in Athens, and that's quite enough.
  What sort of life is this that you lead here
Among the birds? You know it well by now.

HOOPOE

Not bad; at least it whiles away the time.
Firstly, one has to live without a purse.

EUELPIDES

Well, that clears much bad coinage out of life.

HOOPOE

We feed in gardens on white sesame
And myrtle and poppy seed and bergamot.

EUELPIDES

I know; the stuff they scatter upon bridegrooms.

PITHETAERUS

Aha!

[*Suddenly breaking out.*

Ah, yes! By all the gods, a grand idea!
I see a future for the race of birds,
And such a chance of power that might be yours
For ever, if you'll trust yourselves to me.

HOOPOE

What would you have us do?

PITHETAERUS

Well, first of all,
Don't just go fluttering all about the place
With open mouths. It's not respectable.
At home, if you see people fluttering
Like that, and ask why, anyone will tell you
"That's just the Treasurer, Teleas, a bird-man
With no foundation, always on the hop,
Unsettled, never for two hours the same."

HOOPOE

By Bacchus, yes! Your criticism is just.
But what would you have us do?

PITHETAERUS

Build one great city.

HOOPOE

We birds? What sort of city could we build?

PITHETAERUS

You ask that?—Is he blind beyond belief?—
Look down.

HOOPOE

I'm looking.

PITHETAERUS

Now look up!

HOOPOE

I'm looking.

PITHETAERUS

Now turn your head right round.

HOOPOE

And will it do me
Much good to have a dislocated neck?

PITHETAERUS

Did you see something?

HOOPOE

Just the clouds and sky.

31

PITHETAERUS

And isn't that great Whole the bird's estate?

HOOPOE

Estate? How do you mean?

PITHETAERUS

Their place, their land.
And since it's holy, and all existing things
Move through it and in it, it's well named the Whole.
Make it your state and fence it with a wall,
You'll turn it from a hole into a home.
You'll rule mankind like gnats and cockchafers,
And with a Melian famine starve the gods!

HOOPOE

How?

PITHETAERUS

Well, the air, I take it, is mid way
From heaven to earth. Now when we want to go
To Delphi we go first to the Boeotians
For permits to pass through. The same with you.
When men send sacrifices to the gods
Through chaos, which is neutral territory,
Not one whiff of burnt meat will you let through
Unless the gods pay you a fixed commission.

HOOPOE   [*Slowly taking it in.*

Wh-ew! Whe-ew! O Mother Earth! O glory!
Ods nets! Ods traps! Ods limes! Ods devilments!
The neatest, prettiest plot I ever heard!
I'll join you in the founding of that City—
That is, of course, if the other birds agree.

PITHETAERUS

Who will explain the matter to them?

HOOPOE   You.

They used to be barbarians, but I've taught them
Our language, this long time I've lived with them.

PITHETAERUS

Can you somehow collect them?

HOOPOE   Easily.

I'll slip at once into the thicket here
And waken into song my nightingale.
I'll call as well. I warrant, once they hear
Us two, they'll all come running.

PITHETAERUS

                    Best of birds,
Don't waste a minute! Into the thicket quick,
I beg you, and wake up your nightingale.

[*Exit* HOOPOE.

HOOPOE   [*From within.*

My woodland mate, away with sleep!
  Let loose those waves of sound divine
That living in thy memory keep
  The long-lost Itys, mine and thine.
Thy brown throat trembles with its flood
  Of hidden song that, rising, cleaves
  Clear passage through the tangled leaves
Of bind-weed to the realm of God;
Where Phoebus lifts a golden crest
  In joy, and strikes the ivory lyre
  To wake the Muses' answering choir,
Till, through immortal lips expressed
In flow divine is joined with thine
  The rapture of the Blest.

[*Music of flutes. The Hoopoe returns.*

EUELPIDES

Zeus! Such a sound from such a little bird!
It fills with honeyed sweetness all the grove.

PITHETAERUS

Look out!

EUELPIDES

  Why, what's the matter?

PITHETAERUS

          Hush!

34

THE BIRDS

EUELPIDES

What for?

PITHETAERUS

The hoopoe's just preparing for a song.

HOOPOE

Hoo-hóo! Hoo-hoo! Hoo-póo-poo-poo! Poo-póo!
Hum Húm! Come Hum! Come-húm-come-cóme-
    come-cóme!
      Hither gather, gather hither,
      Every brother of my feather;
      Ye that haunt the planted acres,
      Barley-snatchers, blossom-takers,
      Darting wings and melting voices,
        Myriad tribes among the wheat;
      Ye that round the furrow twitter,
        Tweet! Tweet!
      Every chirper, every flitter,
      Each whose little heart rejoices
        High and sweet!
      Tío tio tío tio! Tío tio tío tio!
      Ye who on the ivy branches
      In the gardens hold your dances
        Come along! Come along!
      Ye that round the uplands hover,
      Olive-pecker, strawberry-lover,
       Hasten flying to my song.
      Trioto trioto totobrix!

Hither, ye who make your own
   Earth's well-watered dells and hold
The lovely mead of Marathon;
Hither all; and thou begin,
   Bird with wings of dappled gold,
     Francolin, Francolin!

Divers that over the flower of the sea
Flit with the halcyons, gather to me;
List to the news that is shortly to be,
   The wonderful, wonderful word!
For we are the great World Conference, we,
   Of every long-necked bird.
A dry old man, but modern in mind,
And full of a plan of the modernest kind,
   Is here, and seeks to be heard.

               [*Distant cries of birds*

Tóro toro tóro toro tix. Kikkabow. Kikkabow
Toro tóro toro tóro lililix.

EUELPIDES

Do you see any birds?

PITHETAERUS

      By Zeus, not I,
Tho' I'm agape and staring at the sky.

36

Euelpides

Was it in vain our Hoopoe to that bush
Retired and spouted like a water-thrush?

Flamingo   [*Entering.*

Torotix, torotix!

Euelpides

Hullo there! Look, there's something coming. What
the . . . Yes, a Bird it is.
A bird for certain, but what sort? It's not the famous
peacock, this.

Pithetaerus

The Hoopoe'll tell us if we ask. That one, what sort
of bird is he?

Hoopoe

Oh, he's exotic, not the sort of local that you daily see.
He comes from the great marshes.

Pithetaerus

He's a beauty, coloured all like flame.

Hoopoe

Of course. What else would you expect? Flamingo is
his rightful name.

[*Enter a second oriental-looking Bird.*

37

EUELPIDES

Hi there, look out!

PITHETAERUS

"Why callst thou, varlet?"

EUELPIDES

Here's another fowl close by.

PITHETAERUS

Another? Yes, and one that holds "a strange and
ominous seat on high"
"Who art thou, prophet of the Muse, thou mountain
bird of mysteries?"

HOOPOE

This sort is what is called a Mede.

PITHETAERUS

A Mede you say? Lord Heracles,
A Mede, and yet he travelled here without a camel!
Well, I'm blest.

EUELPIDES

I see another. Here he comes. He's collared a strategic
crest.

[*Enter a third Bird, with a strange crest.*

38

PITHETAERUS

Why, what is this amazing fowl? A Têreus? Is there
    more than one?
Aren't you the only Têreus?

HOOPOE

                This is Philoclês's Hoopoe's son,
And my grandson. You know how names from
    grandfather to grandson pass,
First Callias, then Hipponîcus, then a second Callias.

PITHETAERUS

Then this is really Callias! Poor thing, have all his
    feathers failed?

HOOPOE

Well, being of good birth and rich, by all the informers
    he's blackmailed,
And pretty hen-birds help to pick his last remaining
    feathers out.

    [*Enter a fourth Bird, fat with white feathers.*

EUELPIDES

But here's another, bless my soul, this creature with
    the painted snout;
What do you call this bird?

39

HOOPOE

The Great White-feathered Guzzler is his name.

EUELPIDES

Then has our great Cleônymus a twin? Or are they
both the same?

PITHETAERUS

If he's Cleônymus at least he might have thrown his
crest away.

EUELPIDES

But what's the meaning anyhow of all this crested
war-array?
Are we to have an armoured race?

HOOPOE

No, all our birds go helmeted.
They cling to crests, as Carians do. We think it's safer
for the head.

[*Enter* CHORUS *in a mass.*

PITHETAERUS

But what a plague of birds it is, all round! Poseidon,
how they swarm!
Just birds and birds!

Euelpides

A perfect cloud. Apollo shield us from all harm!
So many of them flapping round, a man can't see
   what's coming in.

Pithetaerus

That one's a partridge, I should say.

Euelpides

And over there a francolin.

Pithetaerus

And here's a many-coloured duck.

Euelpides

And there a halcyon with a frill.

Pithetaerus

And who is that behind her back?

Hoopoe

A barber fowl, the razor-bill.

Pithetaerus

Do fowls have bills and razors?

HOOPOE

Both are met with in a barber foul,
Called Sporgilus. An owl is next.

EUELPIDES

And who to Athens brings an owl?

HOOPOE

Reed warbler, crested lark, blue jay, wood pigeon,
    turtle, spotted flyer,
Gerfalcon, ring dove, cardinal, great cuckoo, red
    shank, crest of fire,
Green woodpecker, great diver, thrush, hawk, water
    wagtail, lammergeier.

EUELPIDES

Oh, the birds! Oho, the blackbirds! How they pipe
    and trot and fuss,
Each one louder than his neighbour . . . You don't
    think they're threatening us?
I believe that's what they're after. Each has got one
    eye on you,
One on me, with beaks wide open; how they stare!

PITHETAERUS

I think so too.

Leader

Whó-hoo Who-hoo cúc-cuc-called me? Where's his
feeding-place or nest?

Hoopoe

Here I am, your friend as always, never failing at a test.

Leader

Tí-ti-tip me then your tiding; is it what a friend's
should be?

Hoopoe

Two wise humans here I've seen.

Leader   [*Startled.*

What? Where? How do you mean?

Hoopoe

Listen! Two men, elder statesmen, have just laid
before my eyes
Highly confidential blue-prints of a marvellous enterprise.

Leader

Oh, you've made the greatest mischief ever seen
beneath the sun!

43

HOOPOE

What is that you say? Don't tremble! Listen!

LEADER

Oh, the wrong you've done!

HOOPOE

I've received two men who love us, and desire our life
    to share.

LEADER

You have done this thing? You've done it?

HOOPOE

And I'm glad I've done it. There!

LEADER

They're already here to-day?

HOOPOE

As sure as I am; and to stay.

LEADER

Woe is me!

44

THE BIRDS

Chorus A

Oh, it's monstrous! We're betrayed.
     He who pecked his worm beside us
In the meadow and the glade,
     Has denied us, crucified us!
The old Rule, the ancient token,
The great Bird Oath, he has broken!
     Lured me to a pit of scorn,
     Flung me out to beasts unclean,
     Who my bitter foes have been
From the day that I was born!

Leader

But him we'll deal with later on. We'll first do justice
     on these two.
We'll peck them into little bits.

Pithetaerus

Indeed? That's bad for me and you.

Euelpides

It's all your fault. It's you alone that brought us to this
     misery.
Why did you ever bring me here?

Pithetaerus

I need a boy to wait on me.

Euelpides

It makes you laugh to see me weep.

Pithetaerus

Weep? How absurd! It's surely plain
They're going to peck out both your eyes, you'll
never, never, weep again.

Chorus B

Ho, forward by the left, Advance!
A deathly cloud above them fling.
Make all your wings about them dance!
Surround them! Wrap them in a ring!
We soon shall hear their dying squeak
And make them fodder for the beak.
No shadowy mountain shall there be,
No skyey cloud, no foaming sea,
Shall ever to these rascals bring
A shelter to escape from me!

[A battle-dance begins.

Leader

Come, let us make no more delays. Have at the rascals!
Tear and bite.
Where has that corps commander gone? Lead forward.
Charge them on the right.

46

THE BIRDS

EUELPIDES

Oh, here it comes. Where can I fly, God help me?

PITHETAERUS

Hold your ground, old man.

EUELPIDES

I won't be pecked to bits. I'll run, I'll fly.

PITHETAERUS

Do you suppose you can?

EUELPIDES

I don't know . . . I've no plan at all.

PITHETAERUS

Well, I can show you in a jot.
We both must hold our ground and fight, each firmly
    clinging to his pot.

EUELPIDES

A pot? What good is that?

PITHETAERUS

At least no Attic owl will peck at it.

EUELPIDES

No owl, but all these birds of prey?

PITHETAERUS

Quick from the scabbard draw your spit.
Plant it before you in the ground.

EUELPIDES

What is there to protect my eye?

PITHETAERUS

Look in the basket. You'll find there a porridge-bowl
or soup-dish. Try.

EUELPIDES

You are a man of brain! Well found! Why, what a
strategist you are!
You quite outrival Nikias in new-found instruments
of war.

[*Each makes the large pot his shield, holds the spit
in the position "to receive cavalry," and puts
on the bowl as a helmet.*

CHORUS

Ha-hah! To battle! Lower beaks! Now let them have
it fast and hot.
Now pluck, peck, tear and flay! But first to breach or
undermine the pot!

THE BIRDS

Hoopoe

Oh, stop and think, you foolish beasts, you creatures
    destitute of wits,
Explain why in the world you want to peck and kill
    and tear to bits
These two Athenian gentlemen, who never harmed
    you in your life,
And happen to be my in-laws, the tribe and kindred
    of my wife?

Leader

These humans, aren't they worse than wolves?
    Imagine, if we let them go,
What beast deserves more punishment? Where can we
    find a fouler foe?

Hoopoe

But what if, tho' by race they're foes, they're really
    friends in mind and mood?
What if they've made the journey here to teach you
    something for your good?

Leader

What could they teach? How could they come to do
    us good, as you aver?
You can't think what foul enemies they were to my
    old grandfather!

49

HOOPOE

Ah, but the wise know how to learn from enemies
    and gain their ends.
Precaution is what saves a state, and that you'd never
    learn from friends,
While enemies compel you to. If cities learn to build
    a wall
And make expensive battleships, their friends don't
    teach them that at all,
It all comes from their enemies. And those are just the
    lessons which,
Once learnt, keep safe your family, your house, and
    all that makes you rich.

LEADER

It may be really of some use to hear what tale they have
    to tell.
One might learn from these enemies some ruses that
    would serve us well.

PITHETAERUS

"Meseems their fury doth abate!" Platoon, two paces
    to the rear!

HOOPOE   [*To Leader.*

That's wise, and only fair as well. For this you owe
me thanks, my dear.

THE BIRDS

LEADER

We do, sir; and we always have obeyed your counsels,
    have we not?

PITHETAERUS

They look more peaceful than they did. Yes, they're
    improving. Ground the pot!
        Then each his bowl to earthward roll,
        And close behind his shield patrol,
        With spit in rest and cautious eye,
        Just, just, above the rim to spy.
        But watch! For we must never fly.

EUELPIDES

    True; but where, suppose we die,
    Shall our heroic ashes lie?

PITHETAERUS

    Why, clearly in the Potters' Row
    The city must a tomb bestow,
    When once we let the Generals know
    How, all surrounded by the foe,
    We fought a war of Kite and Crow
        Like men of Orneai.

LEADER

As you were! Pile arms, your peck and your
    squeak
In a soldierly pack, just under your beak!

[*To the Hoopoe.*

And now, please tell us about these two,
Who the Devil they are or aren't;
Where do they come from and what do they
want?
Hoopoe, we're speaking to you.

HOOPOE

To me? Well, what do you want me to say?

LEADER

Who are these people and whence do they come?

HOOPOE

Two guests of mine, who have broken away
From Hellas, the centre of art.

LEADER

That's rum!
What turn of fortune has set them astray
To the kites and crows?

HOOPOE

A desire most true
For the way you live and manage your day.
They are simply longing to dwell with you,
And live the life you're accustomed to.

THE BIRDS

LEADER

What do you mean? What ground do they give?

HOOPOE

It's a wonderful story. You'ld never believe.

LEADER

Does he see some trick for serving his ends
    By living with me and lingering here?
For downing his foes and relieving his friends?

HOOPOE

    No; he just brings one splendid idea.
You'ld never have thought it, but everything's yours,
The east and the west, the north and the south,
The far and near,
All you can see; he simply pours
The wealth and the power of it into your mouth

LEADER

A lunatic, I should have said.

HOOPOE

A brain incredibly smart!

LEADER

Has he really a brain in his head?

53

HOOPOE

He's a fox, the perfection of art,
All plan, trick, dodge, device and scheme, and purged
    in every part!

LEADER

Of course he must be heard.
    Make him stand up and utter.
Really, your present word
    Puts me in quite a flutter.

HOOPOE

    [*To two slaves who come out from the House.*
Come, you and you! Collect this armament,
Put it to hang again, and luck go with it,
Up in the chimney, near the crockery-stack.
        [*The slaves take the arms away.*
    Now, you explain. Teach them the solemn purpose
For which I called them here.

PITHETAERUS

            Not I, by Apollo!
Not till they grant me a clear covenant,
The same that poor small ape—I mean the one
Who keeps the swordsmith's shop—got from his wife:
No bite, no scratch, no digging with the beak
Below the belt—and that includes the eyes.

LEADER

That I accept.

Pithetaerus

Confirm it with an oath.

Leader

I swear; if faithful, may I get the prize
By vote unanimous of all the judges
And all the audience; if I break my word,
Then . . . just by a majority of one!

Hoopoe

Oyez, Oyez! The heavy armed brigade,
Dismiss! Now for the present go on leave,
But keep your arms beside you, and meantime
Watch for my orders on the notice boards.

Chorus A

A thing of craft and trickery,
    At every hour, in every way,
Man is, and must by nature be:
    Still, say your say.
May be you've hit on something good
That I've not seen or understood,
Or some new source of power divined
Not dreamed of by my simple mind.
    Come, let the public see
    This plan on which you've hit;
    If it brings good to me
      You'll have your bit.

LEADER

I'll never break truce, so don't be afraid, but boldly
    proceed to unravel
The scheme that induced you, whatever it was, to
    start on this venturesome travel.

PITHETAERUS

I'm only too eager to speak, and I've got my matter
    well salted; so now
It's ripe to be kneaded and pressed into shape. Ho, boy
    there! A crown for my brow!
You others, some water to pour on my hands.
    [*The two slaves bring a garland and a basin of
        water.* PITHETAERUS *formally washes his
        hands and puts the garland on his head.*

EUELPIDES

Are we going to have dinner, or what?

PITHETAERUS

Why no, but by Zeus, I'm warming a speech, a large
    one, luscious and hot,
Which will ravish the hearts of all hearers; my own
    so bleeds for you and your fall.
To think that of old you were kings!

LEADER

Us Kings? Why, what were we kings of?

THE BIRDS

PITHETAERUS

Of all!

Yes, all that there is; of me and of him; of Zeus, that
usurper so bold.

You are older in birth than Cronos himself, more
prime than the Titans of old,

And the Earth.

LEADER

And the Earth?

PITHETAERUS

By Apollo, you are.

LEADER

That is something I never had heard.

PITHETAERUS

You are not educated. You never inquire. Of your
Aesop you don't know a word.

He says in his book that the first thing alive was a lark.
All lonely she flew,

Before even the Earth, till her father took ill, and
died on her out of the blue.

And no earth was there, so she sat in despair while for
five long days he lay dead,

Till at last she thought best to develop a crest and
bury him there in her head.

57

EUELPIDES

Is that what the great first Father of larks amounts to,
 a mere dead head?

PITHETAERUS

Then doesn't it follow, since older they are than the
 gods, yes, older than earth
If the laws of primogeniture hold, the Kingdom is
 theirs by birth?

EUELPIDES

Then the first thing for you to devote yourself to is
 growing a beak of your own;
Great Zeus of the Oak won't find it a joke when the
 Woodpecker sits on his throne.

PITHETAERUS

And further to prove that it wasn't the gods but the
 great bird chieftains of yore
Who were rulers of men and legitimate kings, there
 are facts I could give you galore.
Of the Persians, for instance, it's known that a cock
 was the first king, ages ago,
With rank far over Darius the Great and old Mega-
 bazus and Co.
Isn't "Persian Monarch" the name of a cock? That
 comes from the days of his pride.

THE BIRDS

EUELPIDES

The same with his manner. A true Great King you
    can see in his strut and his stride.
And alone of all birds he carries of right his tiara erect
    on his head.

PITHETAERUS

Why, the power he wielded of old was so strong and
    so universally spread
That all folk still obey him and spring to their work
    at sunrise as soon as he crows,
All tinkers and tanners and potters and bakers and
    cobblers and bathmen, and those
Who buckle our bucklers and torture our lyres, while
    some have to get on their toes
And start in the dark!

EUELPIDES

Ask me about that! I lost my best mantle that way,
All Phrygian wool. I had gone up to town for a feast
    on some child's Tenth Day,
And had taken a drop, and before supper came, fell
    asleep; and a cock went and crowed.
And of course I thought it was dawn, and set off for
    my home on the Halimus Road,
And had scarcely peeped out when a man with a club,
    a night-prowler, caught me a whack,
And I fell, and before I could get out a shout
    he peeled off the cloak from my back!

PITHETAERUS

The kite, too! Over all Hellas the Kite was formerly
master and king.

CHORUS

All Hellas?

PITHETAERUS

And that's why they bow to the ground for
the first Kite seen in the spring.

EUELPIDES

Why, yes; at the sight one day of a kite to the earth
I obediently dropped
And swallowed the small change I had in my cheek;
so I left all my shopping unshopped!

PITHETAERUS

In Egypt, however, and Sidon and Tyre, the King
was the great Cuckoo,
And, as soon as for food the cuckoo cuckooed, through
all those countries they knew
They must off to the fields, as the barley and wheat
would be ripe for gathering then.
So complete at that time was the rule of the Birds that
if ever a king among men,
Agamemnon, suppose, or his brother, arose in some
particular spot
On the top of his sceptre they posted a bird, to share
any tribute he got.

THE BIRDS

EUELPIDES

Ah, yes; that bird! I never had heard of it. No, I was
    tempted to laugh
At the play when some tragic King Priam came out,
    with a bird on the top of his staff;
But of course he was watching Lysicrates here, for
    a share in some little blackmail.

PITHETAERUS

Then Zeus, who is now chief Lord of the world—
    this proves my case without fail— .
To show he is king, for his own special bird has an
    Eagle to sit on his mace,
His daughter an owl, and Apollo a hawk, to suit his
    subordinate place.

LEADER

Yes, by Dêmêtêr, it's certainly so, that rule. But how
    came it in use?

PITHETAERUS

It's the wish of the birds, when the worshippers come,
    and lay in the fingers of Zeus
Their gift of burnt meat, to be sure that the god can't
    get at it quicker than they.
Then no one at that time swore by the gods; by the
    birds they did, every day,
As for Lampon "By goose" does instead of "by Zeus"
    when he swears some mystical lie.

So vastly, we're told, did the nations of old respect you
    as holy and high!

    And now you are imbeciles, niggers and drones;
    When you perch in a temple, they pelt you with
        stones,
    As if you were madmen; and everywhere
    Is a fowler with booby-trap, lime-twig and snare,
    With his nooses and springes and gauzes and nets
    There's never an end to the traps that he sets
    Then they sell you; and sell you in dozens at that;
    And the purchasers pinch you to see if you're fat
    Then they eat you, of course; but surely, at most
    They might serve you up as a decent clean roast;
    No; smearing cheese, vinegar, oil, they will come
    At last to that stinking Arabian gum,
    And stir it and pour it, hot, greasy and sweet
    On You—as if you were just dead meat!

                [The Birds are deeply affected

CHORUS B

    How sad, how more than sad to me,
    O Man, is this strange history
    You bring us! How I weep for this
    Proof of my parents' cowardice!
    Just in my day to cast away
    The glories that their fathers gave!
    And what a strange coincidence,
    Or what a gift of Providence,

I'ld rather say, that here to-day
You come to teach us and to save!
Henceforth obedient in your hand
My chickens and myself I lay,
And here shall be your fatherland.

LEADER

Well, now it's for you to say what we must do,
    for life is to me nothing worth
Unless we recover by hook or by crook
    our sovreignty over the earth.

PITHETAERUS

Very good. My first word to you then is UNITE.
    One city of Birds you must fix
And fortify, Babylon-like, with a wall
    of superlative sun-dried bricks.

EUELPIDES

O Giant of Giants, O whale among fish,
    What a city to frighten the chicks!

PITHETAERUS

And when once it is up, tell Zeus to restore
    his usurped crown; send him a mission,
And if he says No and doesn't consent,
    and at once realize his position,

63

Establish against him a Holy Crusade;
    and prohibit those rascals above
From crossing your air to get down to the earth
    on their errands of vagabond love,
To a Semele here and an Alope there,
    or Alcmêna, and so without end.
Then again to mankind I have it in mind
    a co-ordinate mission to send,
To instruct them to sacrifice first to the birds,
    since the Birds are now kings of the sky.
Later on, if they like, to the gods; but with each
    they must find the right bird to supply.
If you want Aphrodite, the Love-bird should first
    have some wheat dedicated, for luck;
Give Poseidon his lamb; but some barley, be sure,
    you must consecrate first to the Duck.
At Heracles' worship the Cormorant claims
    some large stiff honey-cakes, hot;
Zeus, being a king, has a ram as his right;
    but a bird king must not be forgot.
King Fisher demands at his altar the blood
    of a prime gnat, male, without flaw.

EUELPIDES

Great Zeus, a gnat's blood at the altar is good;
    Now thunder and grind your jaw!

LEADER

But will man ever treat us as serious gods,
    and not flibbertigibbets at best,
When we all have wings and just flutter about?

THE BIRDS

Pithetaerus

Oh, absurdity! What is the test?
Isn't Hermes a god? He flies and has wings;
    and lots of those worshiped above.
Doesn't Victory fly on her pinions of gold?
    And the prince of all fliers is Love.
And Iris, as Homer says, goes to and fro
    with a gait like the flight of a dove.

Euelpides

Doesn't Zeus the most High, when in anger, let fly
    his bolt on a fiery wing?

Leader

But suppose in their ignorance men don't see
    that we birds are any great thing,
And stick to the present Olympian gods?

Pithetaerus

An army of sparrows at need,
And seed-peckers, down from the heavens will pounce
    on their fields and gobble the seed.
And then, when they're hungry, Dêmêtêr of course.
    Is bound to provide them with bread!

Euelpides

She's officially bound; but she's sure to be found
    providing excuses instead.

PITHETAERUS

Then crows from the skies will peck out the eyes
 of the poor little cattle that go
With the plough in the field, if still they won't yield,
 and the sheep's eyes too; that'll show!
And Apollo, the Healer, can heal them again.
 He is paid for it. That's only fair.

EUELPIDES

Ah, wait a bit, hold till my cattle are sold,
 my own little, poor little, pair!

PITHETAERUS

But if they accept you as God, Life and Time,
 God of earth and of sea and of sun,
All good things and sweet shall be laid at their feet.

LEADER

All good things? Tell me of one.

PITHETAERUS

Well, first, in their vineyards the bloom of the vine
 no locust army shall eat.
One levy of kestrels and owls is enough
 to inflict on them utter defeat.
No more shall the gall-bugs and gall-bug ants
 on the fig-tree branches be seen.
One bevy of thrushes will come from the Birds
 to lick up the lot of them clean.

66

THE BIRDS

LEADER

But where shall we find them riches and gold?
    For that's what they want, if I know them.

PITHETAERUS

When they come to your shrines, just think of the
    mines that your birds will infallibly show them.
And they'll keep the man-augur correctly informed
    of the best expeditions for gain,
So that none of the skippers will ever be lost
    at sea.

HOOPOE

How so? Pray explain.

PITHETAERUS

There'll be always a bird to reply when they ask
    of the man-augur whether to sail.
"Don't venture to-day. There's a storm on its way."
    "Sail now. It is luck without fail."

EUELPIDES

I am buying a boat. I'm away and afloat!
    I'll stay with you lubbers no more.

PITHETAERUS

Then treasures you'll show buried deep long ago,
        in secret by misers of yore;
The birds best know where such treasures lie low.
        How often the boast has been heard,
"No soul can have seen where I buried my stuff,
        unless peradventure a bird."

EUELPIDES

I'll let the boat go, get a pick and a hoe
        and dig up the pots as I'm shown.

LEADER

But what about health? Can they promise man that?
        The Olympians say it's their own.

PITHETAERUS

When a man's doing well you can certainly tell
        he's in pretty good health.

LEADER

                        'Pon my soul,
At least if a man's "Doing badly" it's true
        you can't call him happy and whole.

LEADER

But how will they ever attain to old age?
        That's a gift for Olympus to give.
Must they all die in childhood?

THE BIRDS

PITHETAERUS

                    Not so; if they want
    three hundred years extra to live,
The birds will provide them.

LEADER
                Where from?

PITHETAERUS
                            Where from?
From themselves. Doesn't every one know,
As the lives of full five generations of men
        is the life of the croodling crow?

EUELPIDES

Hurrah! Hurrah! More worthy by far
Than Zeus to be Kings of the World they are!

PITHETAERUS

More worthy indeed! On that we're agreed.
With the birds for our masters there'll never be need
To pile up temples of ponderous state
With marble walls and a gilded gate.
For house and home it will suit them well
In a bush or a thicket of oak to dwell,
And for even the grandest of birds there'll be
Temple enough in an old olive tree.
We'll make long pilgrimages no more
To the sands of Ammon or Delphi's shore;

Just where we happen to be we'll stand,
Where the self-sown olive and arbutus grow,
Some grains of barley or wheat in our hand,
And lift up an arm to the sky, and so
Pray for some shred of the joy they know.
And quickly, quickly, will joy be born,
At the cost of a few little grains of corn.

LEADER

O once most hated of elderly men, but now un-
    speakably dear,
I'll never desert you; to all your advice I solemnly vow
    to adhere.

CHORUS

Your words have uplifted me now to declare
An unchangeable purpose, and solemnly swear,
If purely, honestly, innocently,
A firm alliance you make with me
To front the Olympians, you and we
Together in an amity for everyone to see,
Not long shall Zeus be unshaken in his powers
And go meddling with the sceptre that is veritably ours!

LEADER

Whate'er can be done by strength alone can be left
    to us birds to do,
But for all that ought to have serious thought we trust
    entirely to you.

THE BIRDS

HOOPOE

Indeed, by Zeus, it's not a time to dream
Or meditate on victories to come;
Leave that to Nikias! Quick to work's the word.
But first, pray, come into my nest and share
Such bits and chippings as I have mustered there.
And kindly let us know your names.

PITHETAERUS

                              With pleasure.
My name is Pithetaerus.

HOOPOE

          And your friend?

EUELPIDES

Euelpides from Krîos.

HOOPOE

          Welcome both!

PITHETAERUS

We thank you for your kindness.

HOOPOE

              Then come in.

PITHETAERUS

Let's go together, but you guide us.

HOOPOE

Come.

PITHETAERUS

But . . . I say. Stop! Back water! . . . Here's a problem.
How are we two to live our lives with you,
When you fly and we don't?

HOOPOE

Oh, that's all right.

PITHETAERUS

H'm. What about the fox in Aesop, who
Went partners with the eagle, and was sorry?

HOOPOE

Don't be afraid. There's a strange root we know;
Once gnaw it soundly and your wings will grow.

PITHETAERUS

Then forward! Ah, what's this? A yellow Thracian
                              [*Two slave birds come forward.*
And a dark Semite? Good; take up the luggage.

72

THE BIRDS

LEADER *[To the Hoopoe.*

Oh, please! It is you that I want.

HOOPOE

What for?

LEADER

When you take these strangers away,
To your great state lunch, don't leave us alone; bring
out your Nightingale, pray,
The sweetest of singers, the mate of the Muse, to be
with us in frolic and play.

PITHETAERUS

By Zeus, a good idea! Please do. Bring out
The shy bird from her covert in the sedge.

EUELPIDES

Yes, by the gods, do bring her, that we two
May see with our own eyes your Nightingale.

HOOPOE

By all means, if you wish. Come, Procne dear,
And let the visitors have sight of you.

[Enter Nightingale.

PITHETAERUS

O Zeus in glory! What a lovely bird,
Such gold too, like the Blessèd Parthenos.

EUELPIDES

Could I . . . I might, I think, give her a kiss.

PITHETAERUS

Deluded man! Her beak's a pair of scissors.

EUELPIDES

Eggs can be shelled. By Zeus, I'll simply peel
Her head-shell off complete, and kiss her so.

[*He does so.*

HOOPOE

Come in.

PITHETAERUS

Lead on. And Fortune with us go!

[PITHETAERUS, EUELPIDES *and the* HOOPOE *go
off through the Door in the Rock, followed by
the Slaves with the luggage. The* LEADER
calls upon the Nightingale.

LEADER

Friend! sweet voice, whom above
All wingèd things we love,
Sharer of all that I sing,

74

My comrade, Nightingale dear,
You have come! You have come! You are here
   In clear vision before us,
Sweet melody on your wing,
And the flute's reawakening;
O living voice of the Spring,
   Give the lead to our chorus!

[*The* NIGHTINGALE *plays a prelude and then accompanies the Chorus on the flute.*

Chorus

LEADER

O Humans, ye natures so dimly alive, like leaves that
   blossom and fade,
Ye little-achievers, creations of clay, impermanent
   tribes of the shade,
Ephemeral, wingless, much-suffering mortals, Men!
   Men that are shapes of a dream,
To Us, the immortal, surrender your minds, Us ever
   alive and a-gleam;
Us, dwellers in heaven, eternally young, whose
   mysteries never shall die,
Till ye learn from our teaching the ultimate truths,
   the secrets of stars and of sky,
The Being of Birds, the Becoming of Gods, Streams,
   Chaos and Erebos; so
You can bid the astronomers shut up their shops, for
   you and you only will know.

There was Chaos at first, and Erebos black, and Night,
and the Void profound,

No Earth, no Air, no Heaven; when, lo, in the realm
of the Dark without bound,

In a vortex of winds the Primordial Egg was engen-
dered by black-wingèd Night;

And out of the Egg, as the seasons revolved, sprang
Erôs, the world's delight.

His back soft-gleaming with feathers of gold, his
heart like a whirlwind storm.

And he with Chaos the wingèd and dark, being mixed
in the Void without form,

Begat the original nestlings of us, and guided them up
to the sun.

The Immortals had never existed at all till Erôs made
all things one.

For at last, as one kind with another combined, came
the Earth and the circling Sea,

And the Sky, and the heavenly race of the Gods ever-
living; but eldest are we,

And foremost of all happy dwellers in heaven; and
verily all things declare

We are children of Love, for we fly as He flies, and
when true lovers meet, we are there.

And pretty young things, at the edge of their bloom,
who have scorned all love as absurd,

A diligent lover can often beguile through the magic
that lives in a bird;

The gift of a quail or a coot will not fail, or a goose, or
a cock in his pride.

Then the things that are most of importance to men
are precisely the things we provide.

It is birds who make clear the chief dates of the year,
of autumn and winter and spring;

The croak of the crow gives a signal to sow, when to
Libya she launches her wing;

It is then that the shipper must hang up his oar: all
winter his hands he can fold;

It is then that Orestes must weave him a cloak; he'll
be tempted to steal if he's cold.

Then later the cry of a kite in the sky, when the
season begins to be fair,

Gives the word for the spring-time shearing of sheep;
and the swallow darts in to declare

That a man will do well his thick woollens to sell, and
buy something light. So the powers

Of all the great oracles, Ammon, Apollo, Dôdôna and
Delphi are ours.

In all undertakings you come for advice to the birds
before anything's done

Be it getting and giving, or earning your living, or
choosing a wife for your son.

In the world of the seer any sign that speaks clear is an
"augury," that is, a bird,

Any opportune sneeze, any sight a man sees on a
journey, a phrase overheard,

A voice at a critical moment, a donkey, a donkey-boy;
doesn't it follow

That for you poor mortals on earth We Birds are the
    real prophetic Apollo?

    Take us for your gods and you'll know how to use
    The wind and the season, the seer and the Muse,
    The winter and summer, the cool and the heat.
We won't go and hide Like Zeus in his pride
    Far off in the clouds on a shimmery seat.
    We'll be with you as friends, and give in good truth
    To yourselves, your sons, and the sons of your sons,
Absolute health, Unlimited Wealth
    And life and peace and laughter and youth,
And festival dances, with food in tons!
Till the Birds' own Milk, with never a hitch,
Comes raining in showers, making all of you rich.

CHORUS A

[The song being interrupted by bird-cries on the flute.

    Muse of the willow copse,
    (Tio tío tio tío tiotinx)
      With whom, deep hid in the dells,
      Or perched in the mountain tops
    (Tío tio tío tio tinx)
      Where the budding ash-leaf swells,
    (Tío tio tío tio tinx)
      I have raised a rippling throat
      To Pan or the Mountain Mother
      For a dance, or a sacred note
      From that field of song, none other,

(Toto tóto toto tóto tototinx)
    Wherein, like a wandering bee,
Old Phrynichus sucked that fruit
    Of melody wild and free
    That filled his lovely lute.
(Tio tío tio tío tiotinx.)

Leader A

Spectators, if you care to spend an easy life from day
    to day
Among us Birds, by all means come and live with us;
    make no delay.
So many things on earth are blamed, or by convention
    vilipended,
Which in the kingdom of the Birds are quite correct or
    even splendid,
By human law, for any son to strike his dad is shocking,
    quite;
Not so with us; he's always free to run up boldly and
    invite
The old bird: "Dadkin, where's your spur! Up with
    it, if you mean to fight!"
A branded runaway with you is treated as a thing of
    shame,
With us he'll be a francolin, branded, but pretty all the
    same.
Another is a "dark Semite," like Spintharus? He
    needn't mind;
He'll simply be a dark Sea-mew—a new one, of
    Philêmon's kind.

79

If he's a waif unparented, slave-born, like Exekestides,
He'll grow white feathers here, and pass as his own
    grandfather with ease;
Suppose that to our outlawed foes the son of Peisias
    should desire
To ope by craft our city gates, true chicken of a
    slippery sire,
A lyre-bird he can be with us. We see great value in a
    liar.

CHORUS B

Thus did the Swans of old
    (Tiotío tiotío tiotinx)
    With music of wings and voice
Where Hebrus river rolled
    (Tíotio tiotio tinx)
    In Apollo's praise rejoice,
    (Tíotio tíotio tinx)
Outsoaring the highest cloud.
    Then cowered the beasts in caves,
    And hushed were the windless waves,
But Olympus echoed loud,
    (Tototóto tototóto tototinx)
And amaze took the Lords thereof,
    As the brood of the mountain side,
    Muses and Graces, cried
In wonder and in love.
    (Tiotío tiotío tiotinx.)

THE BIRDS

Leader B

There's nothing better, nothing sweeter, than with
   wings to pullulate.

For instance, in the audience here if once a man could
   aviate,

Suppose he's hungry and gets tired with long-drawn
   tragic choruses,

He'd just fly up and leave the place, go home, have
   dinner at his ease,

And then when satisfied fly back, and settle down quite
   cosily.

Or think; if Patrocleides were attacked by his
   infirmity,

He need not misconduct himself in public, nor yet sit
   in pain,

He'd fly away and not return till things were all
   correct again.

Suppose there were—there may be—one entangled
   in some love affair,

He'd see his lady's husband safe established in the front
   parterre,

He'd take instanter to his wings, and up, off, down,
   he'd fly; and thus

Secure a private heart-to-heart, and fly contented back
   to us.

To fly, to fly! It's worth the world! Oh, isn't it the
   best of things?

Think how Dieitrephês's wings—just common, low-
   class, wicker wings—

To Captain, then to Colonel raised that nobody, till
    now, of course—
He handles great affairs and ranks High Cockalorum
    of the Horse!

    [*Enter* PITHETAERUS *and* EUELPIDES *with wings,*
        and with feathers painted on their bodies.

PITHETAERUS

Well, so that's that!

EUELPIDES

        Bless me, the funniest thing,
The very funniest thing I ever struck . . .

PITHETAERUS

What are you laughing at?

EUELPIDES

          At your quill feathers!
Do you know what you're like with those things on?
A painted gander, finished on the cheap!

PITHETAERUS

And you, a blackbird with a Newgate fringe!

EUELPIDES

What says the poet? "Eagle, changed thou art
But know, 'tis thine own feathers winged the dart."

LEADER

But now for action!

PITHETAERUS

                   First, to find a name,
Great and resounding, for our City: then
Make offering to the gods.

EUELPIDES

                   I quite agree.

LEADER

Let's think. What shall we make the city's name?

PITHETAERUS

How would you like that name that's the big noise
In Lacedaemon—Sparta?

EUELPIDES

                   Heracles!
A Sparto-city hung on sparto-grass!
Never. I wouldn't leave a truckle-bed
So mattressed, if I had a leather strap.

PITHETAERUS

What shall we call it then?

LEADER

Something from here,
From clouds and heavenly regions, some inspiring
Large name.

PITHETAERUS

Well, what of Cloudcuckopolis?

LEADER

Hurray! Hurray!
Right as a trivet! Simply great and splendid!

EUELPIDES

Is this the land of flying clouds that holds
The ancestral acres of Cleocritus
And Aeschines'· whole fortune?

PITHETAERUS

Best for them
Would Phlegra's Plain be, where the gods outdid
The Giants in the art of the long bow.

LEADER

A splendid thing, our city! And who shall be
Its heavenly patron? Who shall wear the Robe?

EUELPIDES

Athena, Guardian of the Wall; why change?

PITHETAERUS

What law and order could that city keep
Where a mere female goddess stands in arms
Holding a spear—and Cleisthenes his knitting?

LEADER

A Stork Wall we must have; who'll be its Keeper?

PITHETAERUS

A bird we have, of Persian ancestry,
World-famous as the very prettiest fighter,
A chick of Ares!

EUELPIDES

O my patron chick,
Won't he be godlike, perched above the rocks!

PITHETAERUS

To work now! [*To* EUELPIDES] You, walk out upon
    the air,
Stand by to help the builders of the wall,
Strip; then bring out the rubble, knead the mud,
Carry the hod up, tumble off the ladder,
Get the guards posted, keep the fire banked up,
Carry the bell round, camp upon the wall;
Then send one herald to the gods above
And drop another on mankind below,
Then, back to me!

85

EUELPIDES

   Oh, yes; and you wait here,
And put your head in a bag and report to me!

PITHETAERUS

My good man, do! Go where I ask you to.
Without you nothing will get done at all.

        [*Exit* EUELPIDES.

 Now for the sacrifice to our New Gods.
I'll call the Priest who leads the state procession.
Ho, boy! The basket and the lustral water.

        [*He goes into the House.*

CHORUS A

 My voice accords, my will agrees,
 I fully approve your new decrees;
 We'll march in pomp, with solemn pace,
 And bring to the gods, to ensure their grace,—
  A little bit of roast meat, please!
Up, up the empyrean Set afloat the Delphic paean,
  And let Chairis go on piping at his ease.

[*Attendants bring a goat for sacrifice, a basket and
  a lustral bowl, preceded by a Crow playing
  the flute.* PITHETAERUS *returns with a*
  PRIEST *and Acolytes.*

THE BIRDS

PITHETAERUS

Stop blowing, there! O Heracles, what's this?
"Things many and terrible these eyes, y-wis,
Have seen ere now," but never chanced upon
A crow with a musician's mouthpiece on!
Priest, it's for you to make our sacrifice
To the New Gods.

PRIEST

I'll make it in a trice.
Where is the acolyte who bears the basket?

[*He takes a wreath from the basket, crowns himself
and intones.*

Lift up your voices to the Central Hearth of the
Birds, and to the Kite who Guards the Hearth, and
to all Birds and Birdesses, in Olympus and the
Ladies' Annex, and to the Stork Athenaean and the
Hawk of the Sunian Rock . . .

PITHETAERUS

Hail Sunian Hawk! All hail, most virgin Stork!

PRIEST

. . . To the Swan Pythian and Delian, and to Leto
the Partridge-Mother and to Goldfinchian
Artemis . . .

PITHETAERUS

It's not her hair now, it's her finch that's golden!

PRIEST

And to Sabazios of Chaffinchland and the Great Hen,
Mother of Gods and Men . . .

PITHETAERUS

Hail, Cybelê, hen that laid Cleocritus!

PRIEST

We beseech you, grant to the Citizens of Cloudcuckopolis health and security, for themselves and the
Chians . . .

PITHETAERUS

I like the Chians added everywhere.

PRIEST

I call also to such birds as are Heroes or Sons of Heroes,
the purple Coot and the Pelican and the Spoonbill
and the Firefinch and the Heathcock and the Peacock
and the Teal and the Bittern and the Heron and the
Plunger and the Blackcap and the Titmouse . . .

Pithetaerus

Confound you, stop! Stop calling! Wretched man,
Think to what sort of banquet you are inviting
All these sea-hawks and vultures! Can't you see
One kite could fly away with all we've got?
Be off from here, you and your holy ribbons!
I'll carry out this sacrifice myself.

[*Exit* Priest; Pithetaerus *takes the basket and
proceeds to crown himself.*

Chorus B

Once more with hymns and a sacred air
Your sacrifice we must help prepare,
While over the lustral bowl we call
"Come, O ye Blessèd—but, please, not all!
One'll be enough for the fare."
For this animal we've got Most assuredly is not
Much beyond horns and hair.

Pithetaerus

Now pray, and offer to the feathered gods . . .

[*Enter* Poet, *a thin man with long hair, in a
ragged tunic.*

Poet   [*Half chanting.*

To the clime of the cloud,
To the world of the wing,
O Muse, cry aloud
In sweet music, and sing
To the New Gods' blessing and glory . . .

PITHETAERUS

>What *is* this preposterous thing?
Who are you?

POET

>A holy thrall
Of the Muses, from whom shall flow
The honey-sweet rise and fall
>Of verse . . . (That's Homer, you know.)

PITHETAERUS

If you're a thrall, who lets you wear long hair?

POET

>Ah, no; not so!
A poet, whom they call
The Muses' holy thrall:
>(Homer, you know.)

PITHETAERUS

Your cloak is rather holey. That seems true.
What mischief, my good poet, brings you here?

POET

I've written songs for Cloudcuckopolis,
Lots of them, beauties, some made specially
For dances in a ring, and some for Choirs
Of Maidens, others like Simonides.

PITHETAERUS

When did you make these songs? How long ago?

POET

Oh, ever so long! I've always praised this city.

PITHETAERUS

Bless me, isn't to-day its birthday feast?
I've scarcely given the infant child a name.

POET

Swift is the Muse's fire,
As the flash of a racing steed.
"O Founder of Etı. Sire,
Whose very name ina
Standeth for sacrifice,"
Give, Oh, give and rejoice!
As may thine heart incline
Give me, give mine, give thine!

PITHETAERUS

This creature'll end by being a perfect pest
Unless we give him something and get free.
                                    [*To an attendant*
Here, boy! You've both a tunic and a cloak;
Strip off the cloak and make the accomplished poet
A present . . . Keep this cloak, sir. You appear
Still to be somewhat suffering from cold.

91

POET

The gracious and belovèd Muse
This offering slight will not refuse;
Yet in thy mind rehearse,
O man, great Pindar's verse:

PITHETAERUS

The man will never leave us any peace!

POET   [*Knowingly.*

"Where roams the Nomad Scyth
    Outcast he wandereth
Who round his form no loom-wrought vesture
        folds";
    Without a tunic, lo,
    Graceless a cloak shall go;
Rede thou the riddle my sweet music holds!

PITHETAERUS

I "rede" that you expect a tunic too.
                        [*To the attendant*
Well, strip it off. All men must help a poet.
                        [*To the Poet*
Now take it and begone.

POET

I go my ways,
And, going, sing again your city's praise.
　　Muse of the golden throne,
　　Glorify, of thy grace,
　　This shuddery shivery place,
　　　Ochone, Ochone!
　　To a plain by winds through-blown,
　　A region of pelting snow,
　　I came . . . and off I go!
　　　　Tol-de-rol!　　　[*Exit* POET.

PITHETAERUS

Upon my word? Well, surely you've escaped
Our chills by now, with that smart cloak and tunic.
It's something one could never have expected,
The speed with which that pest got wind of us.
　　[*Enter* PROPHET, *carrying a book, i.e. a papyrus
　　　roll.*
The circuit again, boy! Take the lustral water.
Now, silence all!

　　[*The Attendants bring the water and the sacri-
　　　ficial Goat.*

PROPHET　　　[*Coming forward.*
Touch not the sacrifice!

PITHETAERUS

Who may you be?

PROPHET

A prophet, an expert

In oracles.

PITHETAERUS

Well, no one wants you here.

PROPHET

Blasphemer, make not light of holy things!
There is a word of Bakis pointing straight
At Cloudcuckopolis.

PITHETAERUS

Then why on earth
Was I not told of it in time, before
I built the city?

PROPHET

The god held me back.

PITHETAERUS

Ah, well. We'd better hear the holy words.

PROPHET

[*Reading from the roll.*

"Lo, when ravening wolves shall habit with elderly
   ravens
"Housed as one in the realm that Sicyon parts from
      Corinthus . . ."

94

PITHETAERUS

What has Corinthus got to do with me?

PROPHET

In Bakis it's a symbol for the air.

[PITHETAERUS *shrugs his shoulders.*

"First let a white-haired ram be appointed to great
    Pandora,

"Then, who cometh the first to reveal my oracular
    wisdom,

"Grant him a mantle unworn and a couple of brand-
    new slippers . . ."

PITHETAERUS

And slippers too? Not really?

PROPHET

                Take the book!

"Yea, and a bowl well-filled, and of roast meat all he
    can carry . . ."

PITHETAERUS

He says roast meat too, does he?

95

PROPHET

Take the book!

"All this do as I charge you, O youth belovèd of
heaven.

"Great as an eagle in clouds shall you be; but, alas, if
you give not,

"Eagle you never shall be, nor woodpecker, no, nor
titmouse!"

PITHETAERUS

That's really in the oracle?

PROPHET

Take the book!

PITHETAERUS

[*Taking the papyrus roll.*

It seems quite different from this other one,
Which I took down straight from Apollo's lips.
"When at the feast sacrificial an uninvited impostor
"Comes interrupting the service and hopes for a share
of the victuals,
"Deal to him under the ribs of stripes a suitable
portion."

PROPHET

I think you are talking nonsense.

THE BIRDS

PITHETAERUS

Take the book!

"Deal and stint not at all, no, not to an eagle in heaven,
"Not though he prove to be Lampon, or even the
great Diopeithes."

PROPHET

That's really in the record?

PITHETAERUS

Take the book!

[*Beating him with the roll as he comes to take it.*
Out to the carrion crows!

PROPHET

Hi! Murder! Help!

PITHETAERUS

And trot your oracles off to where they are wanted.

[*Exit* PROPHET. *Enter from the other side* METON,
*the scientist, with rules, compasses and other
geometrical instruments.*

METON

I have come in person . . .

97

PITHETAERUS

Here's another pest.
Come to do what? What's the first concept? what
The subsequent review? And why on earth
Do you walk in buskins like a tragic actor?

METON

I purpose to subject the atmosphere
To geometrical measure, and divide it
In acre lots.

PITHETAERUS

In God's name, who are you?

METON

Who am I? Sir, I am Metôn, a name known
In Hellas . . . and Colônus.

PITHETAERUS

Tell me, though,
What are those things?

METON

Aerial measuring rods.
For instance, since the atmosphere in shape
Is like a conical extinguisher,
I place this curvilinear measuring rod
Above, insert a pair of compasses . . .
You follow?

THE BIRDS

PITHETAERUS

Not a bit!

METON

Applying then
A straight rod, I proceed with measurements
Until your circle grows into a square;
The centre of the quadrilateral is
The market-place, and towards that centre run
Straight roads centripetal; just as a star,
Being itself by nature circular,
Has radiating from it rays of light
Quite straight in all directions.
      [*He hands* PITHETAERUS *the large wooden com-
      passes.*

PITHETAERUS

What a Thalês
The man is! . . . Meton!

METON

Yes?

PITHETAERUS

I am your good friend.
You know that. Let me give you some advice.
Move off the road a little.

METON

Why, what's wrong?

PITHETAERUS

Well, it's like Sparta. There's an epidemic
Of xenophobia; violent incidents
In some parts of the town.

METON

Some civic discord?

PITHETAERUS

No, no; quite the reverse.

METON

What is it then?

PITHETAERUS

A harmony of hearts for kicking out
All humbugs.

METON

H'm. Perhaps I should retire?

PITHETAERUS

Do; though I'm not quite sure you'll be in time.
Those "violent incidents" . . . Look! Here they are.

[*Beats him with the compasses.*

100

METON

Oh, mercy! Help!

PITHETAERUS

Ah, well, what did I say?
Now, please, geometrize yourself away.
[*Exit* METON. *Enter* COMMISSAR.

COMMISSAR

Where are the chief Receptionists?

PITHETAERUS

Who's this?
The Great Panjandrum?

COMMISSAR

I am the Commissar,
By lot appointed to report upon
This new foundation, Cloudcuckopolis.

PITHETAERUS

Who sent you here?

COMMISSAR

Some scrubby document
[*Hands a large parchment roll to* PITHETAERUS.
Drawn up by Teleas.

101

PITHETAERUS

Ah; perhaps you'ld like,
Without the trouble and the waste of time
Inspecting, just to take your fees and go?

COMMISSAR

By all the gods, I would. I did, you know,
Petition for a permit to remain
At home and do some work in the Assembly.
The fact is, I have had some confidential
Relations with the satrap Pharnakes . . .

PITHETAERUS

Come, take your fees and leave us; here they are . . .
[*Beats him.*

COMMISSAR

What's this?

PITHETAERUS

Assembly notes on Pharnakes!

COMMISSAR

All bystanders, bear witness! I am assaulted,
A Commissar with diplomatic rights!

PITHETAERUS

Shoo! Shoo! Be off, you and your ballot-boxes.

[*Exit* COMMISSAR, *left.*

This is too much. They send a Commissar
To inspect us and report before we've even
Completed our baptismal sacrifice!

[*Enter (right)* LAW-MONGER, *with a roll of laws.*

LAW-MONGER

[*Reading to himself.*

"And if a citizen of Cloudcuckopolis commits an
offence against a citizen of Athens . . ."

PITHETAERUS

What's this? Another nuisance? What's the book?

LAW-MONGER

I'm a Law-merchant, come to sell a list
Of new laws, bye-laws, rules, decrees . . .

PITHETAERUS

A what?

LAW-MONGER

[*Reading.*

"The people of Cloudcuckopolis to use the following
standard weights, measures and regulations, as
used by the Delians . . ."

PITHETAERUS   [*Taking the roll.*

Yours will be pretty soon more like the Squealians . . .

LAW-MONGER

Man! What's come over you?

PITHETAERUS

You and your laws!

[*Beats him.*

To-day you'll see some laws that you won't like.

COMMISSAR   [*Returning.*

I summon Pithetaerus on a charge of assault and battery before the April sessions.

PITHETAERUS

What's that? [*Turning*] Hullo, are you still waiting there?

LAW-MONGER

[*Returning on the other side.*

"And if anyone attempts to deport an authorized official and fails to receive him in the manner prescribed . . ."

PITHETAERUS

Confound it! Were you too here all the time?

COMMISSAR

I'll ruin you! Damages ten-thousand drachmae. . .

PITHETAERUS

I'll ruin your two ballot-boxes first.

[*Exit* COMMISSAR, *left.*

LAW-MONGER

You recollect the offence that you committed
Behind that public monument after dark . . .

PITHETAERUS

Pah! Seize him someone. Stop, you rascal, you!

[*Exit* LAW-MONGER *right.*

Let's get away withindoors, quick; and pay
The gods the sacrifice they need to-day.

[*Exit* PITHETAERUS *with attendants and the* GOAT.

CHORUS A

All things I see;   All realms I sway;
All men to me   Just dues must pay
With a ritual of humble veneration.
O'er all the earth   My rays I shoot;
I watch from birth   All flowers and fruit,
And make war on the abominable nation
Of guzzlers found   Half-hid in boughs
Or underground,   Who browse and browse
On the berries and the blossoms as they spring.

I firmly kill   The pests that meet
To work their will On gardens sweet;
The things that bite And things that crawl
By ancient right   Are slaughtered all
And die beneath the beating of my wing.

Leader A

So be it; but to-day there is the ancient proclamation
    made;

Whoever kills Diagoras, the Melian miscreant, shall
    be paid

One talent; and whoever kills some Tyrant, now
    deceased, the same.

Additional to which ourselves do now our City's laws
    proclaim;

If someone kills Philocrates, the birdshop miscreant,
    he shall score

One talent in reward, but if he brings the villain living,
    four.

He threads his chaffinches on strings and sells them
    seven to the obol;

He blows his thrushes up with air, all puffed and fat,
    for men to gobble.

He pierces blackbirds' noses with the birds' own
    feathers; baser yet,

He uses pigeons as decoys, his prisoners, helpless in a net.

This we proclaim; and furthermore, if any in this
    place there be

Who keeps birds tethered on a string, we here command
    him: Set them free!

106

If these commands you disobey, a thousand birds shall
       swoop on you
And bear you off to cages here, as our decoys, in
       vengeance due.

Chorus B

Oh, full of grace   Beyond all words
I hold the race   Of wingèd birds,
Who never need a muffler when it's freezing;
       And, much the same,   In stifling heat
       When rays like flame On humans beat
I never find it warmer than is pleasing.
       The meadow's breast   With blossoms clad
       Will shade my nest   When, sunshine-made,
The Chirper of the noon shouts delight.
       In winter's cold   With Oreads gay
       In caves I hold   Our rounds of play:
       In spring time I   Am myrtle-fed
       In gardens by   The Graces spread,
And I peck the little berries, fat and white.

Leader B

One word about the prize to-day. I think the Judges
       ought to know
What blessings, if they vote for us, we birds are ready
       to bestow,
Far greater gifts, I warrant, than those goddesses to
       Paris gave.
We'll give them that which, in their hearts, all prudent
       Judges really crave;

Owls that will never let you down, large silver ones,
    Laureion's best.

They'll take a lodging in your house and in your
    purses build a nest,

And rear a family and hatch small silver owlets from
    the shell.

Then more like temples of the gods shall be the homes
    in which you dwell.

We'll raise your roofs up, eagle-wise, in pediments
    with sloping wings.

Have you an office, and a chance to pick up small
    unnoticed things?

We'll send a young sharp-sighted hawk to teach you
    how—and where—to prey.

You're at a feast? We'll give you crops, like ours, to
    store the cakes away.

But if you don't decide for us, you'ld better get the
    smiths to beat

Some metal haloes for you, like the sacred statues in
    the street.

A man without one, when some day he wears his best
    new tunic . . . why

He'll feel the wrath of all the birds in blobs of vengeance
    from on high.

[*Enter* PITHETAERUS.

PITHETAERUS

My birds, the omens of our sacrifice
Are good. But is there still no messenger

Come from the wall to give us a report
How things go there? . . . Ah, here comes someone
    running
Lord, how he pants, like an Olympic racer!

        [Enter MESSENGER, *panting with haste.*

MESSENGER

Where is he? Where, where is he? Where, where is
    he? Where
Is royal Pithetaerus?

PITHETAERUS

        Here I am.

MESSENGER

Your wall, sir, is completed.

PITHETAERUS

        That's good news.

MESSENGER

It's splendid, great, supermagnificent.
I tell you, on that wall Theogenês
Could meet Proxenidês of the Long Bow,
Each with a chariot and a pair of horses
As big as . . . Oh, the Wooden Horse of Troy,
And each drive past the other without touching,
So wide it is.

PITHETAERUS

By Heraclês, what width!

MESSENGER

And as for height, I measured it myself,
Six hundred feet!

PITHETAERUS

Poseidon, what a height!
But who could build it such a size as that?

MESSENGER

Just birds, no others. Not a bricklayer
From Egypt, not a carpenter was there
Or mason; by their own machinery
They did it all; it filled me with amaze.
From Libya came some thirty-thousand cranes,
Their crops well ballasted with corner stones,
Which sharp-beaked water-rails were chiselling smooth.
Meantime ten thousand storks were making bricks,
While gully-fowl and other river birds
Brought water for them from the earth below.

PITHETAERUS

Who carried up the clay?

MESSENGER

       Herons with hods.

PITHETAERUS

With hods? How was the clay got into them?

MESSENGER

Ah, there they had a really bright invention.
The geese went digging with their feet, like spades,
And shovelled up the clay into the hods.

PITHETAERUS

"O foot of fowl—what canst thou not achieve?"

MESSENGER

And ducks, too, with their coloured aprons on,
Carried the bricks, and swallows close behind
Brought in their mouths the trowel and the clay,
Like bricklayers' boys.

PITHETAERUS

       Amazing! After this
Why should we ever want hired labourers?
But wait a moment. What about the timber?
Who did the wooden parts?

MESSENGER

Bird-carpenters.
Accomplished woodpeckers pecked out the gates
With their own beaks; oh, such a noise there was
Of pecks and hammers, like a naval dock!
So now it all is gated well with gates,
Bolted with bars, secured on every side.
The guards are visited, the bell passed round,
The sentries set, and night-watchers disposed
In all the towers. I must away and wash!
What further should be done is yours to do.   [*Exit.*

[PITHETAERUS *stands silent in thought.*

LEADER

Sir, Sir! What is it? Are you in amazement
To hear of this completion of the wall,
So swift and sudden?

PITHETAERUS

By the gods, I am,
And well I may be. Really these plain facts
Seem more like the invention of a poet! . . .
But who comes here? Some Warden of the Wall
At top speed, with a war-dance in his eyes.

[*Enter* SECOND MESSENGER.

MESSENGER

Hi! Hi! What ho there! To the rescue! Help!

PITHETAERUS

Well, what's all this?

MESSENGER

An outrage on the city!
Just now one of the gods, the gods of Zeus,
Flew through our gates into the atmosphere.
The jackdaw guards, our day-watch, never saw him.

PITHETAERUS

Oh, deed of daring lawless and profane!
Which of the gods?

MESSENGER

We don't know. He had wings;
We know that.

PITHETAERUS

Quick then! Marshal the Home Guard
At once upon his track.

MESSENGER

We have sent a force
Of thirty-thousand falcon sharpshooters;
And every citizen who owns a claw,
Kite, kestrel, buzzard, falcon, night-jar, eagle,
Is out and searching for that god. The sky
Is shaking with the rush and whirr of wings.
He can't be far; he's somewhere hereabouts.
By this time.

Pithetaerus

It's a case for slings and bows.
Attendants, hither all! Take up your bows;
Prepare to shoot. Ho, batman, where's my sling?

> [*The Attendants produce slings and bows.*

Chorus A

'Tis war to the last degree,
Hotter than tongue can tell,
Begins for the gods and me!
Be ready, and guard full well
This cloud-girt atmosphere
Begot of the Darkling Powers.
No god shall take ambush here,
Here, where the watch is ours!

Leader

Watch, everyone! Look all round everywhere.
A wingèd whirling tremor fills my ear
As of some flying god . . . Hah, there he comes!

> [*Enter on a flying Mêchanê,* Iris, *her robes un-dulating and her head surmounted by a rainbow halo.*

Pithetaerus

Hi there, young woman! Where are you flying to?
Stay still! Be quiet! Keep just where you are,
And stop that racing . . . Now, who are you? Name
And nationality? State where you come from.

THE BIRDS

Iris

Where from? I come from the Olympian gods.

Pithetaerus

What do you call yourself? Are you a boat?
Are you a hat?

Iris

Iris the swift.

Pithetaerus

The swift?
Clearly a boat. Excursion or police?

Iris

What does this mean?

Pithetaerus

Some buzzard must fly up
And seize this person.

Iris

Seize me? What's the meaning
Of this annoyance?

Pithetaerus

H'm, you will pay for this.

115

IRIS

Of all the extraordinary . . .

PITHETAERUS

By which gate
Did you, with criminal intent, invade
Our city?

IRIS

Gate? Good gracious, I don't know.

PITHETAERUS

You see her game! Affecting ignorance.
Did you apply to the jackdaw guard? No answer?
Then have you a sealed permit from the storks?

IRIS

What is this madness?

PITHETAERUS

No? You haven't got one?

IRIS

You are in your right mind?

PITHETAERUS

Did no wing-commander
Admit you to the City's liberties?

IRIS

Liberties, sir, are what I don't allow.

PITHETAERUS

And then you are found in silence flying through
A foreign city and the encircling void!

IRIS

Where else do you expect the gods to fly?

PITHETAERUS

That's no concern of mine. They can't fly here.
You are breaking law even now ... Do you understand?
You are caught, and if you met with your deserts
There never was an Iris who more justly
Would die the death.

IRIS

I couldn't, I'm immortal.

PITHETAERUS

That can't be helped. You would. A monstrous scandal
I call it, if to-day when we're established
As rulers of all else, you gods proceed
To misbehave yourselves, and cannot learn
That in due course you must obey your betters.
Tell me, to what port do you steer those wings?

IRIS

I? To mankind, bearing my sire's command
To pay due worship to the Olympian Gods,
Lay sheep and oxen on the altar fire,
And fill the streets with fragrance.

PITHETAERUS

Gods? What gods?

IRIS

What gods? To us, of course, the gods in heaven.

PITHETAERUS

You think you *are* gods?

IRIS

Are there any others?

PITHETAERUS

The Birds are now the true gods of mankind.
Birds have the altars now, by Zeus, not Zeus.

IRIS

[*Descending to the stage.*

O madman, madman! Rouse not the dire wrath
Of Heaven, lest Justice upon all your race
Bring down the mattock of the avenging God,
While your live flesh and home-encircling walls
Red smoke shall shrivel with Licynmian blast.

PITHETAERUS

Listen to me, young woman! Stop that bluster,
And please keep still! What sort of Wop or Dago
D'you take me for, I wonder, that you try
To frighten me with that old bugaboo?
I warn you, if Zeus means to annoy me further,
"The walls and roof-tree of Amphion's house
With fire-fraught eagles I will burn to dust."
I'll send a flight of sea-porphyrions at him,
Up where he lives, the greater spotted kind,
Six hundred of them. Wasn't there a time
When one Porphyrion made him think a bit?
As for his little message girl, you'll find
Old as I am, I'm man enough for her!

IRIS

Wretch, may that wicked language burst your throat!

PITHETAERUS   [*Driving her off.*

Shoo, chicken! Shoo! Be off there quick! Slap, Bang!

IRIS   [*Weeping.*

I'll tell my father how you treated me,
Then you'll be sorry!

PITHETAERUS

                Shall I really? Well,
Fly away now. See if your pretty ways
Will touch the feelings of some younger man.

                [*Exit* IRIS *on her flying mêchanê.*

Chorus B

Away from our land, away,
Zeus and his gods are barred!
Never shall he or they
Traverse our city's guard!
Never, never again
Shall the odour of sacrifice
Have passage through my domain
To the gods of the upper skies!

Pithetaerus [*Gazing off.*

It is odd about our Herald to mankind;
He went; is the man never to return?

[*Enter excitedly* Herald, *with a gold coronet.*

Herald

Hail, Pithetaerus, Hail your Excellence,
Your Wisdom, your Beatitude, your Slickness,
Your Thrice-beatitude . . . your Wisdom . . . Oh,
Won't someone stop me?

Pithetaerus

What are you trying to say?

Herald

The nations crown you with this golden crown
Of Wisdom; all the tribes of men adore you.

PITHETAERUS

I thank them. What do they adore me for?

HERALD

O Founder of this City of the Skies
Most glorious, you can't think what a position
You have won on earth, or what a multitude
Of Cuckoocloud-lovers you now possess.
Before you built this city, all mankind
Were mad for Sparta; fasted, grew long hair,
Abstained from washing, carried those big sticks,
And Socratized themselves. Now that's all changed.
They've gone bird-mad, do everything for pleasure,
As birds do, imitating all our ways.
First thing when they awake, they fly, like birds,
By law of nature, to the courts they love;
Then to the sweet papyrus shelves; then home
To feed on the last laws and regulations.
When I was there they had got to such a point
Of this bird-mania, quite a lot of them
Had actually adopted names of birds.
One limping shopkeeper was called "The Partridge";
Menippus was "the Swallow"; "One-eyed crow"
Was what they called Opuntius; Philoclês
Was just "the Lark"; Theogenês a gander
Crossed with a fox; "the Ibis" was Lycurgus,
"The Bat" was Chairephon, "the talking Jay"
Old Syracosius; Meidias of course
Was called "the Quail," he looked so like a quail
Beaten for cowardice by a quail-flipper.

For love of birds they all were singing songs
With something stuck in somewhere about sea-gulls
Or doves or geese or swallows, or just wings,
Or anyhow, some flutter of a feather.

There's my report on men; but one thing's certain.
You'll soon have thousands of them swarming here;
Wings and a beak-and-talon way of life
Are what they're clamouring for. You'll have to find
Somewhere or other wings for all your settlers.

PITHETAERUS

By Zeus then, we must not stand idling here.
Quick, Xenthias; fill all the bales and baskets
With wings, and Manes bring them out to me.
I must be ready to receive all comers.

> [*A dance in which the Attendant Birds bring out
> baskets of wings, or sometime loose feathers,
> while Pithetaerus and the Chorus flap and
> beat them with their wings.*

CHORUS

—Man soon will complain in so many words
That it's crowded with men, this City of Birds.
Good luck come with them! For really this
   fashion
Of living like birds is becoming a passion.

PITHETAERUS

Quicker, there; do what I'm telling you to!

Chorus

—Everything beautiful haunts this place
　　To which wandering man may aspire;
Wisdom is here and ambrosial Grace,
And kindly Calm with her sun-lit face;
　　Oh, here is the heart's desire!

Pithetaerus

Was there ever a stupider slave?
Quicker! Quicker! To work, you knave!

Chorus

—Who is it that brings the basket of wings?
　　You hurry him up yet again!
Like this, with a stick, to make him come quick,
　　He's a slow old ass, that is plain.

Pithetaerus

Old Manes is lacking in brain.

Chorus

—Bring pinions of every degree.
　　Arrange them in packages three;
The species that sings, the haruspical wings,
　　And the wings that fly over the sea.

Then you can look at each separate man,
And think how to fit him as well as you can.

PITHETAERUS

Slug! Slow-coach! by the Kites, how can I keep
My pinions off you when you're half asleep?

[*While* PITHETAERUS *is busy with the birds who
are bringing the baskets of wings, enter a*
FATHER-BEATER, *singing.*

I would I were, I would I were,
An eagle whirling through the air,
To thread the unharvested inane
Above the sea-blue swelling of the main!

PITHETAERUS

That herald's story will prove true, it seems;
Here's someone who comes singing about eagles.

FATHER-BEATER

Bird-mad is what I am. I fly! I long
To live with you! I am pining for your laws.

PITHETAERUS

We have many laws; which are you pining for?

FATHER-BEATER

Oh, all; but most especially the one
That says it's brave to bite and choke your father.

PITHETAERUS

Why, certainly, we think it shows great courage
In any chicken to defeat his father.

124

Father-Beater

Well, that's just why I want to move up here,
And choke the old man and have all the stuff.

Pithetaerus

Ah, we've another fundamental law,
Engraved on the ancient tablets of the storks;
That when the father stork, by board and lodging,
Has made all the young storklets fit to fly,
The chicks in turn must board and lodge their father.

Father-Beater   [*Dismayed.*

Good God, I've done a nice job, coming here! . . .
Do you mean, I'll have to board and lodge the man?

Pithetaerus

No, since you are here, young man, I'll help you out.
I'll have you feathered as an orphan bird.
But in your case, young fellow, I would make
A mild suggestion, much the sort of thing
I learnt when I was little. Don't go on
Beating your father. Here are wings for you—
Take them—and in the other hand a spur;
Then make this crest of a prime fighting cock
Your regular wear. Go! First year in a fortress,
Then active service! Earn a soldier's pay,
And make it keep you. Let your father live,
But, since you're such a fighter, don't waste time;
Off to the Thracian front, and fight your fill!

Father-Beater

By Bacchus, yes! I call that good advice.
I'll do it.

Pithetaerus

Then you'll show some sense at last!

[*Exit* Father-Beater. *Enter from the other side
the Lyric Poet* Kinesias.

Kinesias

Gaily I fly Up to the sky,
    Lightly my journey winging.
Ever on strange Ventures I range,
    This way and that way flinging,

Pithetaerus

This thing will need a waggon-load of feathers.

Kinesias

Body and brain Fearless and fain,
    Ever new music bringing!

Pithetaerus

The famous lime-tree man, Kinêsias!
"And whither wilt thou bend thy winding way?"

Kinesias

Make me a bird! Let me be heard
    Clear as a nightingale singing!

PITHETAERUS

No, please stop singing. Tell me what you mean.

KINESIAS

Give me my wings! I want to soar sublime
And gather from the clouds fresh overtures—
Music of rustling air and beating wings.

PITHETAERUS

Can poets get overtures from clouds?

KINESIAS

                              They must.
The essence of our art hangs on the clouds.
The brightest things in any dithyramb
Are airy, darkling, shot with dim blue light
And beating wings . . . You'll listen to some now.

PITHETAERUS

No, that I won't.

KINESIAS

        By Heraclês, you shall!
You'll see me traverse the whole field of air.
"Ye forms of wing-borne racers of the sky,
Swan-throated" . . .

PITHETAERUS

Ease her! Stop her!

KINESIAS

"Oh, to fly
On the welter of the winds to the deep, to the deep,
With a leap!"

PITHETAERUS

You and your wind! I'll calm it in a moment.

KINESIAS

The southward journey may tempt me forth,
Then back I turn to the wind of the North,
But upward, heavenward, fluttering now
A harbourless furrow of air I plough.

[PITHETAERUS *suddenly smothers him with wings
from behind, with feathers flapping.*
A graceful thought, Sir; most intelligent!

PITHETAERUS

Here are your "beating wings." I hope you like them.

KINESIAS

Is this the way you treat the great Conductor
Whom all the tribes are fighting to possess?

PITHETAERUS

Well, would you like to stay with us, and teach
A choir of wingèd birds, the Creakers' choir,
Paid by the slender Leotrophides?

KINESIAS

I see you are making fun of me; but still,
Be sure I'll never rest till I have flown
All winged and feathered, o'er the skyey zone.

[*He retires flapping his wings. Enter from the other
side the* INFORMER. *He looks around con-
temptuously.*

INFORMER

Just a few fowls with speckly wings;
　　Beggars with never a sou!
But I must, I suppose, say the usual things:
　　"Bright Swallow-bird, how do you do,
Child of the spring With wide-spread wing?"

PITHETAERUS

This plague is breaking out on a fair scale.
Here comes a new man, crooning about wings!

INFORMER

Again I remark, Greeting to you!
Wide-winged Swallow-bird, how do you do?

PITHETAERUS

Again? He must be thinking of his cloak.
He knows one swallow wouldn't make a spring.

INFORMER

Where's the official who provides the wings?

PITHETAERUS

Here; but please state exactly what you need.

INFORMER

Wings, wings, of course! Don't ask a second time.

PITHETAERUS

You wish perhaps to fly straight to Pellênê,
To the wool-factory, for a warmer cloak?

INFORMER

Lord, no! I'm a professional informer
And summons-server on the islanders . . .

PITHETAERUS

Indeed. Congratulations on your trade!

INFORMER

And general inquisitor. I want wings
To whizz about the islands everywhere,
City to city, serving summonses.

PITHETAERUS

With wings you'll serve them more artistically?

THE BIRDS

INFORMER

No, I just want to cross the seas untroubled
By pirates and fly back with the autumn cranes,
Crop-filled with prosecutions, just for ballast.

PITHETAERUS

So that's the trade you practise? Speak it out.
A young strong man, you make your living by
Informing against our allies?

INFORMER

               Why, what else
Would you have me do? I never learnt to dig.

PITHETAERUS

Good God, but aren't there other decent trades
In which a man like you can earn a living
By lawful work, not shady lawyer's tricks?

INFORMER

Bless the man, I want wings, not good advice.

PITHETAERUS

Don't my words lend you wings?

INFORMER

             Why, how can words
Lend a man wings?

PITHETAERUS

Always the heart of man
Is winged by words.

INFORMER

The heart?

PITHETAERUS

You've surely heard
Boys' fathers talking in the barbers' shops:
"It's awful how Dieitrephês's talk
Has given wings to my poor boy's ambition
To drive a racing chariot." And a friend
Will answer that his own son has been set
All in a flight and flutter for the stage.

INFORMER

Words, you say, gave them wings?

PITHETAERUS

Exactly so.
By words the mind is sublimated and
The man uplifted. That is my way now;
With wingèd words I wish to make you soar
Right up to a decent business.

INFORMER

Well, I won't.

PITHETAERUS

You won't?

INFORMER

I'll not disown my family.
We've always made our living as informers
From my old grand-dad down . . . Come, fit me out
With wings, light wings, and swift as any falcon
Or hawk. I want to serve my summons there,
In the island; then immediately fly here
And prosecute, and then back there.

PITHETAERUS

I see.

[*Goes as though to get wings and comes back with
a double scourge.*

Your man will be found guilty in default
Before his ship can get here?

INFORMER

That's the talk!

PITHETAERUS

Then, while he's still at sea, you fly back there
To confiscate his land.

133

INFORMER

        Good! You have grasped
The whole plan. I just spin round like a top.

PITHETAERUS

Quite so. I'm rather good at whipping-tops.
By Zeus, and here's the very thing for you,
Corcyra made, two-winged, to make you fly.

INFORMER

Oh, Hell! A whip?

PITHETAERUS

        No, no; two balanced wings,
They'll give you a flying spin this very day.
        [*Beats the* INFORMER *with the scourge.*

INFORMER

Oh, Hell! What's this?

PITHETAERUS

        Wing off! Absquatulate;
Go down the drain, you infernal scoundrel, you!
You'll see what comes of dirty shyster-tricks.
        [*Exit* INFORMER.
Collect the wings there, and we'll go indoors.
        [*Exit* PITHETAERUS *with* ATTENDANTS.

Chorus A

Through strange wild regions we have flown
    And seen how Nature varies.
We've seen a tree, the sort of growth
You'ld never guess, upon my oath,
In gutless foreign soil it's grown,
    Cleonymus vulgaris.
It's use is, it's no use at all!
It's rotten and it's big, that's all.
In spring it dilates and delates,
But when the autumn heat abates
It hurriedly defoliates
    Its shields, and rather bare is.

Chorus B

And near the Dark a land we know,
    The Waste of the Unlighted,
Where mortal men with Heroes meet
Quite safely, and converse, and eat,
In daylight; but beyond, not so;
    If one should be benighted
And in with great Orestes fall,
Ah, then he'd have a stroke, and all
    His right side would be blighted.

[*Enter a figure swathed in wraps, hooded, and
holding an umbrella; it is* PROMETHEUS.

PROMETHEUS

Dear me!
Dear me, I hope Zeus won't catch sight of me
Please, where is Pithetaerus?   [*Enter* PITHETAERUS.

PITHETAERUS

What the Devil
Is this? Who's the big bundle?

PROMETHEUS

Can you see
A god of any sort round here behind me?

PITHETAERUS

No, none. But who are you?

PROMETHEUS

What time is it?

PITHETAERUS

Time? It must be a little past mid-day.
But tell me who you are.

PROMETHEUS

Siesta time,
Or later?

PITHETAERUS

Upon my word, you make me sick!

136

PROMETHEUS

What is Zeus doing? Heaping up the clouds,
Or clearing?

PITHETAERUS

Drat the man, expect the worst!

PROMETHEUS

In that case I'll unwrap.   [*He does so.*

PITHETAERUS   [*Astonished.*

Not our old friend,

Promêtheus!

PROMETHEUS

Hush, hush! Please don't talk so loud.

PITHETAERUS

What is it?

PROMETHEUS

Silence, please! Don't speak my name.
You'll be the death of me if He sees me here.
I've all the confidential information
From up above; and, if you want to hear it,
Take this umbrella, please, and hold it up
Over my head, so that the gods can't see me.

137

PITHETAERUS

Splendid! A wise, a Promethean thought!
Creep under, quick, and boldly say your say.

PROMETHEUS

[*Under the umbrella.*

Now, listen carefully.

PITHETAERUS

Go on; be sure
I'm listening.

PROMETHEUS   [*Whispering.*

Zeus is utterly undone!

PITHETAERUS

Undone? At what time did he come undone?

PROMETHEUS

From when you people colonized the air.
Men have quite ceased to offer sacrifices ·
To any gods; no savour of burnt meat
Has floated up to us since that fatal day.
It's like the Thesmophoria, a strict fast;
No altar gifts; and the barbarian gods
Screeching up there with hunger, like the Illyrians,
And swearing to invade Zeus from the North
Unless at once he throws the markets open,
Lowers all obstacles to trade, and lets them
Freely import their meat and chips again . . .

PITHETAERUS

Why, are there other gods, barbarian gods,
Up above you?

PROMETHEUS

Are there barbarian gods?
Of course. Where else would you expect to find
The ancestral god of Exekestides?

PITHETAERUS

And what's their tribal name, these barbarous gods?

PROMETHEUS

Their name? Triballi.

PITHETAERUS

That whole bally tribe
May hang itself for me.

PROMETHEUS

I wish it would?
But listen; I've one certain piece of news.
Ambassadors are coming presently
From Zeus and these Triballi of the North,
Seeking a truce. Now, don't commit yourselves
To any treaty until Zeus agrees,
First, to restore the sceptre to the Birds,
And second, to assign as wife to you
The Sovereign Bride.

PITHETAERUS

Why, who's the Sovereign Bride?

PROMETHEUS

A maid most fair, who keeps in charge for Zeus
His thunder and all his royal attributes,
Law, counsel, discipline, naval estimates,
Bad language, paymasters and jobs and fees . . .

PITHETAERUS

Why, all political life is in her charge!

PROMETHEUS

That's what I say. If you can once get her,
You'll have got everything. That's why I came,
To make you understand the whole position.
You know I have always been the Friend of Man,

PITHETAERUS

(You gave us wherewithal to fry our fish.)

PROMETHEUS

And enemy, as you know, of all the gods.

PITHETAERUS

(Of course, yes; always an ungodly object.)

PROMETHEUS

An absolute Timon!—I must run back home.
Please keep the umbrella close above my head,

So that, if Zeus should see me from above,
He'll think I'm one of the attendant virgins
Who march in the Panathenaic Feast.

PITHETAERUS

Good! Here's a special throne for you to attend!

[*He sits in the chair, while* PROMETHEUS, *with a servant holding the umbrella over his head, wheels the chair out.*

CHORUS A

Among the dim Skiâpodes,
    Who walk in Shade, there is a lake
Where the unwashen Socrates
        Conjures men's sleeping souls to wake.
'Twas there Pisander came, to search
        If somewhere he could find the spirit
Which, living, leaves him in the lurch;
        He brought a sacrifice of merit
Peculiar, just a camel-lamb,
Faint of heart and broad of ham;
Odysseus-like, he slew it, pat,
And stepped away and waiting sat:
When up out of the dark there swam,
Thirsting to taste that camel-lamb . . .
        Who but Chairephon the Bat?

[*Enter three Ambassadors from Zeus,* POSEIDON, HERACLES, *and a* TRIBALLIAN.

141

POSEIDON

Ah, here's the wall of Cloudcuckopolis
At last, to which we are ambassadors.

> [*Looking round at his colleagues and noticing the*
> TRIBALLIAN.

Now you; what are you doing? All your cloak
Left-shouldered! Throw it over to the right.
What clumsy? Are you like Laispodias,
Left-legged by nature?—Oh, Democracy,
To what a pass you have brought us, when the gods
Elect this creature! [*Arranging him*] There! Can't
   you keep still?
Confound the fellow! Upon my word, you are
The most uncivilized god I have ever seen.
   Now, Heracles, what action shall we take?

HERACLES

I've told you; I say, break the fellow's neck,
Whoever he is, who dares to starve the gods.

POSEIDON

My good man, we were sent here to discuss
Terms of a truce.

HERACLES

         All the more reason that,
I say again, to break the fellow's neck.

142

PITHETAERUS

*[Entering with the cook and attendants, and not
attending to the Envoys.*

Give me the cheese-grater. The Libyan relish!
And more sauce! Blow the charcoal to a blaze.

POSEIDON

[With ambassadorial dignity.

We three, being gods and envoys from above,
Give greetings to the master of this house . . .

PITHETAERUS

[Paying no attention.

See that the Libyan Relish is well grated.

HERACLES

[Fascinated by the sight of food.

What meat is that?

PITHETAERUS

Some oligarchic birds
Who were found guilty of subversive action
Against the Demos and condemned to death.

HERACLES

So you grate Libyan relish over them
Before they're cooked?

143

PITHETAERUS

[*At last looking round.*

Oh, hullo, Heracles!
What is it?

POSEIDON

We are Envoys from the gods
Appointed to hold conference with you
About some termination to this war.

COOK   [*To Pithetaerus.*

This flask of olive oil is empty, Sir.

PITHETAERUS

Oh, that won't do. Game must be cooked with fat.

[*Sends the cook off.*

POSEIDON   [*Continuing.*

Since we get no advantage from the war,
And you, if your relations with the gods
Were friendly, would have adequate supplies
Of rain-water, to keep your marshes filled,
And halcyon weather always. On all this
We come with full powers to negotiate.

Pithetaerus

[At last attending to him.

It never was our people who began
This war against you, and we still are ready,
If even now you will accept fair terms,
To make a treaty. Our fair terms are these.
That Zeus return the Sceptre to the Birds
Forthwith. If on this basis we can make
A treaty of friendship, I herewith invite
The Ambassadors to lunch.

Heracles

That's good enough.
I give my vote . . .

Poseidon

What's that? This is disastrous.
[To Heracles.

Sir, you are a fool, a glutton! You will end
By robbing your own father of his crown.

Pithetaerus

You think so? Won't the real strength of the gods
Be greater if the Birds have power below?
Why, now, when mortals want to swear false oaths
They hide under the clouds and swear by you.
If once you make alliance with the Birds,
When someone falsely swears the twofold oath,
"By Crow and Zeus," a crow will come unseen
And fly right at him, and peck out his eye.

POSEIDON

A good point, by Poseidon!

HERACLES

So say I.

PITHETAERUS

And you?

TRIBALLUS

Yah, all-time upside pidgin, yum!

PITHETAERUS

You see; he too approves . . . But that's not all
The help we'll bring you. Here's another point.
Suppose a man has vowed some god a gift,
Say, of a sheep, and then goes playing tricks,
Saying, "Gods are patient," and from nasty greed
Won't pay you what he owes, in that case too
We'll have it out of him.

POSEIDON

How? Please explain.

PITHETAERUS

When that man's either counting up his money,
Or naked in his bath, a kite will swoop
Down in a flash, and whisk off to the god,
In coin or clothes, the value of two sheep.

[*The Ambassadors talk together.*

146

HERACLES

Again, I vote to give the sceptre back
To these people.

POSEIDON

Well, now ask the Triballus.

HERACLES

Triballus, do you want to go to Hell?

TRIBALLUS

Me backee swish-swish you-fellow. Yah Yum.

HERACLES

He says he perfectly agrees with me.

POSEIDON

Well, if you are both decided, I concur.

HERACLES

I say! We all agree about the sceptre.

PITHETAERUS

By Zeus, there's one thing more I've just remembered.
I waive all claim to Hera. Zeus may keep her.
Only, the Sovereign Bride must be assigned
As wife to me.

147

POSEIDON   [*Indignantly.*

You have no wish for peace!
Let's go straight home.

PITHETAERUS

It's all the same to me.

[*Turning away.*

Remember, chef. This sauce is to be sweet.

HERACLES

Poseidon, my good man! Where are you off to?
Are we to go to war about one woman?

POSEIDON

What would you have us do?

HERACLES

Do? Why, make peace.

POSEIDON

You stupid! Can't you see he's cheating us
The whole time? It's yourself you're injuring.
If Zeus gives up his Kingdom to these Birds,
And then dies, you'll be ruined. Everything
That Zeus leaves at his death belongs to you.

[HERACLES *stands puzzled.*

THE BIRDS

PITHETAERUS

God bless me, how he outmanœuvres you!
Come over here. I want to tell you something.
Your uncle is just deceiving you. Poor devil,
No share whatever in your father's fortune
Is yours by law. You are illegitimate,
Not true-born.

HERACLES

What the blazes do you mean?
I illegitimate?

PITHETAERUS

Indeed you are.
Your mother was an alien. That is why
Athena ranks as heiress. If she had
Any legitimate brothers, obviously
That couldn't be.

HERACLES

Suppose my father left
A special deed of gift, made at his death,
To me, his illegitimate son, by name . . .

PITHETAERUS

The law does not allow him. This Poseidon,
Who puffs you up so now, will be the first
To fix his clutches on your father's fortune,
Claiming to be by law the next of kin.

I'll quote you Solon's law upon the point.
"A bastard has no right of inheritance if there are
legitimate children. If there are no legitimate children
the next of kin share the property."

HERACLES

You mean to say I don't get any share
In my own father's property?

PITHETAERUS

        Not you.
I swear you don't. Look here. Just tell me this;
Has Zeus yet taken you to sign your name.
At the Office of the family Registrar?

HERACLES

Why, no. I often wondered why he didn't.

        [He shakes his fist and scowls at the sky.

PITHETAERUS

What good is gaping at the sky like that?
Do you mean assault and battery? No, no;
Come on our side and I'll establish you
As a true king; I'll give you pigeon's milk.

HERACLES   *[After thinking.*

I think your claim's quite fair on this point too;
About the girl, I mean. I give her up.

PITHETAERUS   [*To* POSEIDON.

And what say you?

POSEIDON

I vote the contrary.

PITHETAERUS

It all lies with Triballus.—What's your vote?

TRIBALLUS

Ver boofer girlie, ver big high-up Missus,
Dis chile say no no birdie gibbum. Yum.

PITHETAERUS

There! Give her up, he says.

POSEIDON

                    He never said so!
Damme, he just goes jabbering like a swallow.

PITHETAERUS

He jabbers you must give her to the swallows.

POSEIDON

You two, then, make your peace and sign your treaty.
You're both agreed, so I say no word more.

HERACLES

We vote for granting everything you want.
Come to the sky. You can collect up there
The Sovereign Bride, and all the other stuff.

PITHETAERUS

How fortunate these fellows were cut up
In nice time for the wedding feast!

HERACLES

                Please, uncle,
Wouldn't you like me to stay here a while,
And see to the cooking? You can go all right.

POSEIDON

The cooking? Good hard eating's what you mean.
You come with us!

HERACLES   [*Sighing.*

    I should have had a time!
   [HERACLES *reluctantly obeys. The three gods return*
    to Heaven.

Pithetaerus

Ho there, ye varlets! Bring my bridal robe!   [*Exit.*

Chorus B

Deep in the dark Informeries,
Hard by the Water-clock, has sprung
A rascal race of savages,
A brood half-belly and half-tongue.
They reap the harvest, sow the seed,
Just with their tongues, and quickly breed
     A crop of Informations.
From alien soil to us they fare,
A Gorgias here, a Philip there.
'Tis surely those embellied tongues
Of Philip and his tribal band,
Have caused the rule through all our land,
That 'mid the sacrificial songs
For tongues a place apart is planned
     From ordinary oblations.
            [*Enter* Herald.

Herald

O everywhere victorious beyond words,
O wingèd and thrice-blessèd race of Birds,
Receive your master to his joyous home!
He comes, more splendid than the stars that roam
In golden fire, and shining at his side—
No sun more full of radiance—see the Bride,

Beauty surpassing speech! And in his hand
The bolt of Zeus, the wingèd thunder-brand!
Through heaven's deep vault sweet nameless odours rise
And wreaths of incense, lovely to the eyes;

> [*Enter* PITHETAERUS *with the* BRIDE *and Atten-
> dants.*

But see, himself is here. O Muse, unseal
Thy lips in purity and words of weal.

CHORUS

Fall back! Open up! Make a front! Give room!
Flutter, ye Birds, round the blissful groom.
His is the fortune, his the bloom.
He has won his bride, a bride to make
Your realm a City of Joyfulness;
Great, great fortunes shall now possess
The City of Birds for this man's sake.
With bridal music, Hymên! Hymên!,
Your master greet and his shining Queen.

CHORUS A

So Hera the Queen of old
And the Lord of the sun-trod throne
Did the Weavers of Life enfold,
'Mid music of mystic tone,
In bridal and joys untold;
    Sing we so!
Hymên! Hymenaeus!

CHORUS B

And He of the wings of gold,
Erôs, the rein did hold,
And the straining chariot guide
With blessing from either side
For Hera, the Fortunate,
Belovèd of Zeus the Great,
    Long ago!
Hymên! Hymenaeus!

PITHETAERUS

In all the music of your voices
And dancing gay, my heart rejoices;
    Your loyal words I praise.
But now is time to make resound
The crash that echoes underground,
The lancèd fire of Zeus, the Sire;
    The levin's fearful blaze.

      [*Thunder and Lightning.*

CHORUS

All hail, thou golden levin-light!
Hail, shaft of Zeus that cannot die!
Hail, thunder of the nether night
That draws the rain-cloud from the sky!
To Him the quaking earth doth groan,
To Him all things divine are given,
And by him, partner of his throne,
The Sovereign Bride, the child of heaven!
Hymên! Hymenaeus!

PITHETAERUS

In and out, in and out,
Wind we now our marriage rout.
Come, ye feathered tribes who share
With me the pastures of the air,
To reach the realm of Zeus, and thread
The maze to that high marriage-bed.
Reach out thine arm, O happy bride,
And lead the dancers at my side.
Then clasp my wing, and lightly cling;
Up, up, above the world we swing!

CHORUS

Paiân! Paiân, and Alalai!
Tênella! Victor of the Sky!
   Hail, O Most High!

P. 16, l. 11. Exekestides: see Note on Persons.

P. 16, l. 14. We hear more of Philocrates's mis-doings below. P. 106, l. 1077. Orneai, cf. *ornis*, "bird," a town near Corinth, chosen here merely for its name.

P. 16, l. 15, Tereus; king of Thrace, and husband of the Athenian princess Procne, by whom he had a son Itys or Itylus. In the common version of the story he violated Procne's sister, Philomela, and the two sisters in revenge killed Itys. As Tereus in rage pursued them they were all transformed into birds; Tereus to a hoopoe or else a hawk, Procne to a nightingale, Philomela to a swallow. In later versions Philomela became the nightingale and Procne the swallow. The nightingale's song, with its repetition of something like "*itu-itu*" is her unceasing lament for Itys, while the Hoopoe, pursuing her, cried "*Pou-Pou*," "Where? Where?"

Homer, however, says she killed Itys "by mistake," which implies a different story. In this play the Hoopoe and the Nightingale seem to be on the best of terms, not as if there was a record of crime between them.

The hoopoe is a bird about 12 inches long, with a brilliant black and white crest, which it opens and closes continually, and a long slender beak. The rest of its plumage is a mixture of black, white, grey and golden buff.

P. 17, l. 28. "Go to the crows," who feed on dead bodies, was a common curse.

P. 17, l. 31. Sakas: The Sakae were Scythians. There is evidently an allusion to someone of doubtful ancestry.

P. 18, l. 43. A pot, etc.: the apparatus for sacrifice; the pot for the fire, the basket for the meat, salt and knife, the myrtle for wreaths. The sacrifice would be necessary for establishing the settlers in a new city.

P. 19, l. 54. There was a proverbial saying, "Kick the rock and the birds will fall."

P. 20, l. 60. The Trochilus is a man dressed up as a bird, like the Hoopoe and the Chorus afterwards. Hence the fright of the two men. The Crow and Jackdaw must have been much smaller. There probably was some comic "business" with these birds, and with the goat at l. 959 ff.

P. 20, l. 62. Fowlers: The first thought of the Trochilus, as of the Chorus later, is that men are the Birds' worst enemy.

P. 21, l. 70. Beaten by some cock: in a cock-fight the beaten bird was supposed to be the slave of the victor.

P. 24, l. 93. Sophocles had recently produced a tragedy, *Tereus*, in which the hero was transformed into a Hoopoe, a thing which obviously invited ridicule. The change was perhaps just indicated by giving Tereus a triple crest but not feathers or wings. Of the effect when Pithetaerus and Euelpides get their wings, cf. p. 82, l. 801 ff.

P. 25, l. 102. Blazing peacock: Peacocks were a rarity in Athens. A certain Demos, son of Pyrilampes, had some and exhibited them once a month. No ordinary bird could be transmogrified into such a figure as this Hoopoe; but a peacock transmogrified ...?

P. 26, l. 109. Jurors: i.e. members of the popular jury courts to which the Athenians were supposed to be so much addicted. Cf. l. 41 above. In Aristophanes' *Wasps* the jurymen are represented as ferocious insects, eager to judge and condemn.

P. 27, l. 125. The name of Skelias' son: his name was Aristocrates. See list of persons.

P. 28, l. 147. The official galley: called Salaminia, which had been sent in the previous year to arrest Alcibiades at the head of his army. See Introduction.

P. 32, l. 186. Melian famine: The island Melos had been reduced by blockade the year before.

P. 33, l. 197. If the other birds agree: The Hoopoe is a strictly constitutional king, like Theseus in tragedy.

Pp. 34, l. 209. My woodland mate: Both here and below, l. 676, we have a song addressed to the Nightingale, while she herself only replies on the flute.

P. 37, l. 267. Flamingo: These four special birds who enter singly were perhaps leaders of the four divisions of the Chorus of twenty-four. There may be some topical joke about the Flamingo and the Mede; if so, it is lost.

P. 38, l. 275. The language shows quotation from tragedy.

P. 39, l. 280. The second Tereus: Philocles, as well as Sophocles, wrote a tragedy *Tereus*. His Tereus was evidently differently got up, and this bird is a travesty of Philocles's Tereus as our Hoopoe is of Sophocles's Tereus.

P. 40, l. 292. As Carians do: The Carians are said to have invented helmets, and in war had a habit of retiring to the "crests" of hills.

P. 42, l. 301. "Owls to Athens": like "coals to Newcastle." The owl was Athena's sacred bird, and was encouraged in Athens. Attic coins were stamped with an owl's head. Of course not all the birds in this list can be identified.

P. 46, l. 348. No shadowy mountain, etc.: a touch of tragic language.

P. 47, l. 358. No owl will peck: no Attic owl would be so unpatriotic as to attack an Attic pot. The two men are armed like Tweedledum and Tweedledee in *Alice*.

P. 49, l. 368. My in-laws: Procne was an Athenian princess.

P. 51, l. 395. The Ceramîcus, or Potters' Quarter, was a burial-place of special honour; the name Orneai suggests *ornis*, a bird; also, there had just (416 B.C.) been a fiasco there; an Athenian army besieged the town, only to find that the enemy, some Argive exiles, had stolen away in the night.

P. 51, l. 401. Your peck and your squeak: as a soldier, at ease, lays down his weapons beside his shield.

P. 54, l. 434. These two slaves, Xanthias and

Manodorus, or Manes (656, 657), probably entered in attendance on the Hoopoe at l. 92.

P. 54, l. 441. That poor small ape: The "ape" who kept the swordsmith's shop is not known.

P. 55, l. 445. To get the prize by a majority of only one is the worst fate the poet chooses to imagine.

P. 57, l. 475. Bury him there in her head: This absurd "Aesop fable" is found also in Indian and Arabic literature, but in both it is told not of the lark but of the large Oriental Hoopoe.

P. 59, l. 487. His tiara erect: In Persia it was the special privilege of the King to wear his tiara upright.

P. 59, l. 494. Tenth Day: the day the child received its name.

P. 59, ll. 495 ff. Night-prowler: Apparently there was an outbreak of assault and theft by night at this time. The culprit was, for some reason, nicknamed Orestes, after the famous mad hero. Cf. 712, 1491. A topical joke of which the point is now lost.

P. 60, l. 499. Bow to the Kite; The arrival of this kite (*milvus regalis*) was a sign of spring. It was welcomed as the cuckoo is with us.

P. 61, l. 515. Birds on sceptres: The Athenians had never seen a king except on the stage. The gods, as is well known, often had special birds associated with them, on their sceptres or heads or hands.

P. 62, l. 526. Pelt you with stones: as Ion does in Euripides' play, ll. 154 ff.

P. 62, l. 534. Arabian gum: Silphium or asafoetida was a common relish.

P. 64, l. 559. Alopê, Semelê, Alcmêna: These unedifying amours of Zeus, as of other gods, come from the habit of each tribe or community or royal house deriving its descent from some local god and heroine. When the local gods were absorbed by, or unified in, the great god Zeus, he was left with a number of local consorts.

P. 65, l. 580. Dêmêtêr . . . provide them with bread: a reference to the state distributions of corn. If Demeter is to act as a "Minister of Food" she will behave like the rest of them.

P. 66, l. 584. Apollo: being the official Healer, presumably gets his salary like other state doctors.

P. 69, l. 609. Five generations . . . the croodling crow: From Hesiod, fr. 171, though there it is nine generations.

P. 71, l. 644. The names: Pithetaerus, "Persuade-companion," has been translated as "Win-friend," which is misleading. Better would be "E. N. Tyser." He is a born *Führer*, who can inspire his *Hetairia*, or band of comrades. Euelpides is simply "Hopefulson." His deme, Krios, means "ram," and perhaps suggests "Mutton Head."

P. 73, l. 670. It seems that the Nightingale comes on wearing a bird mask with a long beak; this has to be removed before she can play her flute, and Euelpides' indiscretion provides a way of removing it. She wears gold ornaments like those on the image of Athena Parthenos (the Virgin).

P. 75, l. 685 ff. O Humans, etc.: The "Parabasis"

(Stepping-forth) of the Chorus is a regular feature of the Old Comedy, in which the Chorus often speaks on behalf of the poet and gives advice on public affairs. Here the Birds speak in their own character as winged prophets, giving an account of the origin of the universe. This beautiful opening passage is a parody of the traditional cosmogonies of Orpheus and Hesiod and various mystics. There is a famous translation of it by Swinburne.

P. 76, l. 695. Erôs: (the vowels pronounced as in "fellows"). In the cosmogonies the primeval Chaos is apt to be brought to some shape either by *Dînos* (vortex) or by Love and Hate, i.e. attraction and repulsion. Here we have the Erôs of poetry.

P. 77, l. 716. Ammôn: (from *ammos*, sand) the oracle of Zeus in the African Desert; Dôdôna: a very primitive oracle in N.-W. Greece.

P. 77, l. 717. Come for advice to the Birds: A great part of ancient seercraft consisted in watching the behaviour of eagles and other large birds and interpreting it. The Latin word "augury" comes direct from *avis*, a bird.

P. 78, l. 738: tiotio-tiotinx: These signs represent bird-cries, probably done on the flute, either interrupting or making a background to the articulate song.

P. 80, l. 774. Hebrus: the river in Thrace, is the traditional scene of the unearthly singing of the dying swan. The Mediterranean swan does give a musical cry.

P. 82, l. 800. Cockalorum: literally, a Hippalectryon, an imaginary Horse-cock or Flying horse.

P. 82, ll. 801 ff. The funniest thing: The poet rather cleverly exploits the inadequacy of his bird-disguise by himself laughing at it.

P. 82, l. 807. Thine own feather winged the dart: A quotation from the *Myrmidons* of Aeschylus, perhaps a self-reproach of Achilles for causing the death of Patroclus.

P. 83, l. 816. Sparto or esparto grass: used either for straw or for a coarse sort of rope.

P. 84, l. 824. Phlegra: mythical scene of the Battle of the Gods and the Giants; the battle in which Aeschinês and Cleocritus excelled would be that of "drawing the long bow."

P. 84, l. 827. The Robe: Borne in the Panathenaic procession and presented to Athena in the Parthenon.

P. 85, l. 832. Stork Wall: Part of the ancient wall of Athens was called either "Pelasgikon," as built by the pre-Hellenic Pelasgi, or "Pelargikon," from *Pelargoi*, storks, who nested there.

P. 85, l. 838. Bird of Persian ancestry: the clue to this allusion is lost.

P. 85, l. 842. The bell: carried round by sentries; if the sound failed it showed that something was wrong.

P. 86, l. 847. Euelpides here disappears for good.

P. 87, ll. 865 ff. The Priest speaks in prose, in parody of the regular official ritual, mixing the names of birds and gods. The *Hestia* (Hearth or central fire) was almost a goddess, like the Roman *Vesta*.

P. 88, l. 880. The Chians: In recognition of their faithful help at the beginning of the Peloponnesian War the Chians had a regular place in the public prayers of Athens.

P. 88, l. 881. Heroes: Some birds being gods, some are naturally heroes or demigods.

P. 90, l. 911. Long hair: a mark of fashion, perhaps in imitation of Sparta.

P. 91, l. 926. Sire whose very name, etc.: A parody of an address of Pindar's to Hieron, tyrant of Syracuse. The adj. *hieros* means "holy." Pindar's appeals to the tyrant's bounty seemed ridiculous and unworthy to democratic Athens.

P. 92, l. 943. No loom-wrought vesture: In Pindar it is "no wain-wrought dwelling." The Scythian nomads lived in caravans.

P. 93, l. 959. PROPHET: The Poet is mocked but treated kindly; the Prophet is the first of a series of humbugs who are beaten with the instruments they themselves bring, the Prophet with his long tight papyrus roll, Meton with one of his instruments, the Commissar with his authorization roll, the Law-monger with his "list." With the scoundrelly Informer it is different (p. 134, l. 1463). This prophet is not a seer (*mantis*) but a professional collector of oracles, generally coming not from Delphi but from some more mystic and less respectable source. These oracle-mongers are a favourite butt of Aristophanes.

The goat is evidently a comic figure.

P. 94, l. 968. The realm that Sicyon parts from

Corinthus: Sicyon and Corinth were conterminous. There was no "realm" between them. The phrase is proverbial. Note that the oracles are all in hexameter verse like Homeric poetry.

P. 95, l. 971. Pandora: That particular goddess is chosen because her name suggests "Give-all."

P. 98, l. 994. First concept ... subsequent review: Probably technical terms in the mouths of scientific philosophers like Meton. "In buskins like a tragic actor": the reading here is uncertain.

P. 98, l. 998. Colônus: As one might say "Famous throughout Europe and Islington." Meton is said to have made some waterworks at Colônus.

P. 99, l. 1009. A Thalês: the famous philosopher: as we might say "What a Solomon!"

P. 101, l. 1021. COMMISSAR: A sort of political inspector, like the Commissaires sent to watch generals in the French Revolution. This man gives himself great airs and brings ballot-boxes to make sure that the new city follows democratic rules.

Panjandrum: literally "Who is this Sardanapalus?"

P. 103, l. 1035. LAW-MONGER or Decree-Monger: In the difficult times during the long war the Demos passed great numbers of laws, regulations, prohibitions, etc., as Aristophanes constantly complains. This man makes collections of them, which he sells as handbooks.

P. 106, l. 1074 f. Some tyrant now deceased: At some religious festivals a commination service was read, pronouncing curses on suitable persons, such as tyrants and atheists. Apparently such curses were apt to be left unchanged and not brought up to date.

P. 106, l. 1085. Set them free: A bird tied with a string, apparently, "sets all heaven in a rage."

P. 107, l. 1095. "Chirper" (*âchetâs*), a pet name for the cicada, like *phereoikos*, "house-carrier," for snail, or our "pussy" for cat.

P. 108, l. 1106. Owls . . . Laureion's best: Attic coins stamped with an owl from the silver mines at Laureion in the south of Attica.

P. 108, l. 1110. Eagle-wise: The pediment of a temple was technically called an "eagle" from some imagined likeness to a great bird with spread wings.

P. 110, l. 1130. I measured it myself: Perhaps a hit at Herodotus, who uses this phrase in describing the measurements of the Pyramids. (Bk. 2, 127.)

P. 110, l. 1137. cranes . . . ballasted: It was a popular belief that cranes used stones as ballast to keep their flight steady. (Also bees, Verg. G. iv, 194.)

P. 111, l. 1147. O foot of fowl: There was a proverb "O hand of man, what," etc.

P. 112, ll. 1164–9. Why should Pithetaerus stand in silent amaze? There is no mechanical necessity, since he might easily have had a dialogue with the Leader to fill up the time while the First Messenger is changing. Perhaps a further hit at Herodotus or some writer who had expressed astonishment at his own story?

P. 114, l. 1198. A wingèd whirling tremor: How does Iris enter? I think, by a *Mêchanê*, like a god in tragedy. This is not explicitly stated, but there are references to the rushing noise, the weapons needed are arrows and slings, the intruder is said to fly. Also the Mêchanê might be taken for "a ship."

P. 115, l. 1204. Excursion or police: Literally it is a choice between two official ships, the *Paralos*, used for festivals and ceremonies, and the *Salaminia*, used for police. It had just been sent to arrest Alcibiades.

P. 119, l. 1244. A parody of Euripides' *Alcestis*, 675. "Do you think I am a Lydian or a Phrygian that you talk like this to me?"

P. 119, l. 1245: That old bugaboo: Iris had been using tragic language, Pithetaerus shows he can do the same. A "Licymnian blast" does make sense, meaning a blast like that which destroyed Licymnius in Euripides' tragedy; the "house of Amphîon" has no relevance at all.

P. 119, l. 1249. The porphyrion was a water-bird, the purple coot; but Porphyrion was a king of the Giants who fought the Gods at Phlegra.

P. 121, l. 1281. mad for Sparta: There were two sources of this "Laconomania." The aristocrats admired the Spartan constitution as well as Spartan discipline and self-control, while philosophers like Socrates, with no thought of politics, became like Spartans through their asceticism. They did not waste time in the public baths or barbers' shops.

P. 121, l. 1287. Courts: The men go by nature to law courts, the birds to garden courts: the men to papyrus books, the birds to beds of sweet papyrus.

THE BIRDS

P. 121, l. 1292. One limping shopkeeper: Peisias. See list of persons.

P. 124, l. 1336. Father-beater: In a primitive society old people depended for support on the "piety" of their children. The obvious way for a young man to be "bad" or "impious" was to treat his old father badly. This man is a selfish young ruffian, but at least an obvious and straightforward ruffian, rather better than the charlatan prophet and much better than the villainous informer. His song is a fragment of Sophocles.

P. 126, l. 1377. Lime-tree man: the point of this epithet is not known. It is a pale light wood.

P. 128, l. 1401. A graceful thought: Kinêsias is first pleased at having the wings, then indignant as he is smothered with them.

P. 128, l. 1404. Kinêsias was a Conductor, or Chorus-trainer: in the competitions each tribe would be anxious to get the best trainer for chorus. "The creakers": a reference perhaps to the bird called *krex*.

P. 129, l. 1410. The Informer, or *Delator*, who looks out for breaches of the law, or invents them, and gets a proportion of the fines, naturally likes to have rich victims. He is at present a poverty-stricken villain in a threadbare coat; but if he had wings. . . .

P. 130, l. 1422. On the Islanders: The subject-allies, many belonging to old cultivated Ionian families were a profitable prey to men of this type.

P. 134, l. 1463. Corcyra-made: The police in Corcyra were armed with long two-tailed whips.

P. 135, l. 1473. A tree: which proves to be

Cleônymus. It *dilates*, i.e. gets fatter and fatter, and *delates*, i.e. is a professional informer.

P. 135, l. 1483. The Waste of the Unlighted: The reference is obscure. Apparently there was some part of the city which was convivial in daylight but particularly dark at night and open to attacks from the robber, "Orestes." Of course there was no systematic street-lighting in ancient towns.

P. 136, l. 1494. Prometheus: The Friend of Man, chained by Zeus on a rock in Mt. Caucasus because he saved man from destruction. To us he is a majestic tragic figure, owing to the work of Aeschylus and Shelley, but it is worth remembering that in Athens he was a local fire-god, the patron of the potters, who shared an altar with Hephaestus in the potters' quarter.

P. 136, l. 1500. Siesta time: It will be safer if Zeus is having his nap.

P. 138, l. 1519. Thesmophoria: A three-day festival of women in honour of Dêmêtêr. The second day was a strict fast, the women sitting as mourners round the statue of the goddess.

P. 139, l. 1529. Triballi: See List. The pun in the Greek is hard to render; Merry suggests something about "tribulation."

P. 139, l. 1536. The Sovereign Bride: The Greek is *Basileiă*, Queen, not *Basileiā* Sovereignty (see l. 1537). Neither we nor Pithetaerus himself have heard of this Basileia before, and the Scholiasts only make impossible guesses. She is clearly not Athena or Hera, and the underworld Basile who was worshipped with Neleus is different in character. For the mystic marriage with the *Basilinna* described in the introduction see Mommsen *Feste der Stadt Athen*, pp. 392 ff., or Deubner *Attische Feste*, pp. 100 ff. The *-inna* termination is ancient, at any rate in Boeotia, and is certainly "hypocoristic." On Dionysus as Young Zeus see A. B. Cook, *Zeus*, pp. 271–91 and Appendix IX G. The form *Basilissa* is late and becomes the regular word for Queen in Macedonian times.

P. 140, l. 1546. To fry our fish: By giving man fire.

P. 141, l. 1553. Skiâpodes: "Shade-footed," indoor people, like women and philosophic students, with pale feet. The name gave rise to a fable of a tribe which shaded itself with its large feet when lying down. Similarly Socrates, who "awakened men's souls," is supposed to be a necromancer who awakens the spirits of the dead.

P. 141, l. 1563. Chairephon, the bat: a worker at night, thin as air and full of fire, he would make just the "spirit" that the fat Peisander needed.

Enter the Ambassadors: How do they enter? At l. 1686 they go up to Heaven; here they have come down from Heaven, though the fact is not explicitly stated. If a *mêchanê* was used for Iris it may well have been used for these gods. Cf. Pithetaerus's final exit.

P. 142, l. 1570. Oh, Democracy: Poseidon, patron of the Knights, is an aristocrat; a greedy Heracles is traditional in comedy; the Triballian an invention of Aristophanes.

P. 149, l. 1652. Mother an alien: The gods evidently

observe Attic Law. Marriage with an alien was not lawful unless there was a special treaty between the two states. Athena was, of course, true Athenian, whereas Alcmena, the mother of Heracles, was Boeotian.

P. 150, l. 1669. Family Registrar: Athenian children were formally introduced to the Phratria, or clan, at the Feast of Apaturia.

P. 152, l. 1692. Heracles: it is not clear whether Heracles obeys or rushes away after the food.

P. 153, l. 1694. Informeries: An invented word, meaning the haunts of informers, near the water-clock which measured the time allowed for speeches in the courts.

P. 153, l. 1696. Half belly and half tongue: Professional orators, like the Sicilian Gorgias, who for a fee would support the informers in prosecuting the innocent.

For tongues a place apart: This was the old custom; now, says Aristophanes, we have learnt what good reason there was for it.

P. 154, l. 1715. Nameless odours: ambrosial fragrances for which mortals have no name. Such fragrance often heralds the advent of a god.

P. 156, l. 1765. O thou most high: On what seems to us the extreme blasphemy of this final scene, see Introduction.

NOTE ON PERSONS NAMED IN THE PLAY

There is much truth in Aristophanes' boast (*Peace*, 751 ff.) that "At women and poor little private men he never railed or cursed." Nearly all the men mentioned in *The Birds* were famous or notorious in political or artistic life. To the artists and poets he is mischievous; new styles in thought or art have always been fair game to the satirist; but as a rule he is kindly also, as he had been to Socrates in the *Clouds* and was to be some years later to Euripides in the *Frogs*; but to the public men who seemed to him like shadows of his old enemy, Cleon, flatterers of the mob, oppressors of the allies, war-mongers, witch-hunters, informers and blackmailers, he is pitiless; and he likes them still less if they have bad manners and no literature.

AESCHINES: nicknamed "Smoke" or "Hot Air"; a great Laconiser, bearded and ascetic; called "son of Sellos" probably with reference to the Selloi of Dodona who "slept on the ground and never washed their feet." Recently envoy to Thessaly; at the end of the war envoy to Sparta; one of the Thirty Tyrants of 404.

ARISTOCRATES: Signed the Peace of 421; in 411 joined Theramenes in setting up the government of the Four Hundred, but finding Critias and his party acting treasonably, helped to overthrow it and restore the democracy; was *stratêgos* with Alcibiades;

commanded a galley at Arginusae and was put to death. Mentioned with respect by Thucydides, Plato and Demosthenes; the disgust expressed in l. 127 applies only to his name.

BAKIS: like Sibylla, originally the name of a class of traditional prophets or supposed authors of oracles; then Bakis, or "the Bakis," was regarded as a particular person. The tyrant Pisistratus was nick-named Bakis, from his interest in oracles.

CALLIAS: son of Hipponîcus, who again was son of Callias: A great Athenian banking family. The younger Callias was a rich pleasure-loving intellectual. In Plato's *Protagoras* he is found entertaining all the most famous sophists of the time. In the *Frogs* he is represented as a lady-killer.

CHAIREPHON: one of Socrates' intimate disciples, noted as particularly intense and enthusiastic by Plato and Xenophon, as pallid, thin and ascetic by the comedians. It was he who asked the Delphic oracle if there was anyone wiser than Socrates and received the answer No one. He differed from most of the circle by being an ardent democrat, which made him a useful witness for the defence in the trial of Socrates. He went into exile during the Rule of the Thirty, returned with the democrats, but seems not to have long outlived the condemnation of his master. In l. 1563 the fat and cowardly Peisander, fishing for his "spirit," which is lost draws up Chairephon, "the bat." He was frail as a spirit and full of fire.

CHAIRIS: a flute-player. He was apt to perform uninvited. (*Peace*, 951.) His unexpected appearance, when someone better was expected, made Dicaiopolis in the Acharnians "die in convulsions." (*Ach.*, 16.)

CLEISTHENES: adopted the Macedonian fashion of going clean-shaven, which in a bearded generation led to obvious jokes. He is like a woman. The Clouds, when they see him, take the shape of women; in the *Thesmophoriazusae* he is among the women as one of themselves; when Mnesilochus, after shaving, looks in the glass he is "just like Cleisthenes." In the *Acharnians* he is called, oddly enough, "son of Sibyrtius," a trainer of athletes (l. 118). But the clue to Aristophanes' hostility is not his shaving habits. In the *Knights* (1374) he is one of the "beardless orators" who must be silenced when Athens is reformed. And Lysias (XXV, 26) calls him an informer. "He is one of a gang of men who . . . have persuaded you to put men to death without trial; who have brought about unjust banishments and confiscations," and so on.

CLEOCRITUS: Archon in 413, and at one time Herald of the Mysteries. A heavy fat man, in shape like an ostrich's egg (877), he might be made to float by having the light Kinêsias tied on to him (*Frogs*, 1437).

CLEÔNYMUS: a sort of Falstaff, but far more sinister. He was one of Cleon's jackals; it was he who moved in 425-4 the doubling of the tribute of the Allies; he proposed a reward of 1,000 drachmae (Pisander made it 10,000) for information about the mutilation of the Hermae, and inflamed the fears of the mob. In the early plays he is just a poor and dirty hanger-on of Cleon's with a great appetite. His signet is "a cormorant on a rock, addressing the public" (*Knights*, 958). Later at some battle or other the fat man dropped his shield and ran away, a ridiculous scene which is never forgotten. He is "this big Jackalonymous dropper of shields" (*Wasps*, 592). He drops his shields regularly in the autumn as plants drop their leaves (1473). In the *Wasps* (l. 19) a man dreams that he sees an eagle catch an asp and carry it high into the air . . . where Cleonymus dropped it! (The Greek word *aspis* means both "asp" and "shield.") Among birds he is identified with the "Great White-feathered Guzzler" (l. 287).

DIAGORAS: A famous philosopher from the island Mêlos, named "the atheist"; to call Socrates "the Melian" (*Clouds*, 830) is a suggestion of impiety. Diagoras was the victim of a religious "witch hunt" and proscribed in Athens about this time. He fled to Pellêne, from which city his surrender was demanded in vain.

DIEITREPHES: A low-class climber, apparently; attacked by other comedians as "a mad Cretan," "scarcely Athenian," and one of a set of "shameless (or "pitiless") beasts." (Cratînus.) He had some military command in Thrace. In 413 his ill-governed Thracian troops broke loose and committed a horrible massacre at Mycalêssus. In 411 he was one of the oligarchs. In trade apparently he had grown rich as a maker of baskets and wicker flasks. A violent and perhaps uneducated man, he seems to have had his admirers; his son had a statue of him set up, dying pierced by many arrows.

DIOPEITHES: A famous prophet or augur. He intrigued against King Agêsilaus in Sparta, and was accuser in the trial of the philosopher Anaxagoras. He charged high fees (*Knights*, 1085). Doubtless he was active now about the Hermae. To Aristophanes he probably seemed a superstitious trouble-maker.

EXEKESTIDES: A man of alien birth, "a slave and a Carian," who had somehow managed to obtain Athenian citizenship; he could find a fatherland anywhere! (l. 11.) The comedian Phrynichus speaks. of "three great apes and bad citizens, Pisander, Teleas and Exekestides, one a coward, one a flatterer, and one a bastard."

GORGIAS: of Leontini in Sicily, came to Athens as an envoy and made a deep impression by his "exotic" style of speech, elaborate, poetical, highly rhythmical, full of metaphors and irony. He settled in Athens and taught a newly discovered subject, the art of speech. As a sophist we have a picture of him in Plato's dialogue, *Gorgias*.

KINESIAS: A favourite butt. He was a dithyrambic poet of the style represented in ll. 1373 ff.; a great innovator; in Pherecrates's comedy *Chiron* the Muse appeals to Justice against his "outrages" and the way he "turns everything inside out." Plato (*Gorgias*, 501) describes him as one of those who "would do anything to please the gallery." He was very thin and looked "almost dead," which was according to Lysias, a punishment for his impiety. He evidently belonged to the new school of music which culminated in Timotheos and which Aristophanes had found excessive even in Euripides. Anyone guilty of dancing his Pyrrhic should be punished in the next world (*Frogs*, 153). The Kinesias of the *Lysistrata* is an imaginary character based on a punning misinterpretation of the name.

LAISPODIAS: As a general he made the first open breach of the truce with Sparta by invading Laconia in 414; afterwards he conspired with the Four Hundred, but was on bad terms with his political comrade, Antiphon, who prosecuted him; went on a mission to Sparta on behalf of the conspirators, but was captured on the way by the Argives and probably put to death as a traitor to the demos. The name suggests "left-footed" or "hairy-legged," and he is said to have worn his tunic long to conceal his legs.

LAMPON: The most famous official prophet of the time. He had a seat of honour in the Prytaneum; was a prime mover of the colonization of Thurii in 444, and his name stood first among the signatories of peace with Sparta in 421. He swore "by the Goose" (*ma ton Chêna* instead of *ma ton Zêna*) to avoid impiety!

LEOTROPHIDES: unknown except for jokes about his
thinness.

LYSICRATES: otherwise unknown. Evidently an official.
Perhaps the same Lysicrates who had a conspicuous
nose and dyed his hair in *Eccles*, 630, 736.

MANES, MANODORUS: slave names, said to be Phrygian.

MEIDIAS: devoted to the sport of quail-fighting;
prosecuted for peculation by a certain Metagenes;
spoken of as an incompetent demagogue in Plato's
Alcibiades: "Think of Meidias, the quail-breeder,
and others like him who manage our politics; in
whom, as the women say, you 'can still see the
slaves' hair-cut' in their minds as well as their
heads, when they come out with their barbarous
lingo to flatter us Athenians, not to rule us."
(*Alc.* 1, p. 120.)

MELANTHIUS: son of Philocles, the tragic poet;
general in 411. Famous for greediness; author of
the prayer "for a throat like a swan or crane," so
as to enjoy his drinks more. He wept at finding all
the best food sold out (*Peace*, 1010). His tragedies
and his voice, "the painfullest I ever heard!"
ridiculed by Aristophanes (*Peace*, 801 ff.).

MENIPPUS: Only mentioned here l. 1293. He is called
"a swallow." Probably as speaking incomprehensibly.
A Menippus proposed a motion to give pardon to
Andocides if he would give evidence against others
concerned in the mutilation of the Hermae.

METON: a great man of science. He devised plans for
water-supply to cities, but is chiefly famous for his

work on the calendar, i.e. the problem of making the sun-cycle and the moon-cycle exactly coincide. In Meton's Great Cycle of nineteen years they did so within some seconds.

NIKIAS: the chief Athenian general in the Peloponnesian War, cautious and generally successful; a rich and generous man, of moderate views and high character. He opposed the Sicilian expedition, but was put in command of it. Fell ill and begged to be relieved of his command, but was defeated with overwhelming loss in 413 and put to death by the Syracusans.

OPUNTIUS: a "snouty man" and "like a one-eyed crow." One would not live in Opus for fear of becoming Opuntius (an Opuntian). Otherwise unknown.

ORESTES: The name of this famous tragic hero was for some reason applied to any nocturnal "Mohawk" or hooligan. It is not likely that one particular garrotter or night-thief infested Athens unpunished from the time of the *Acharnians* (425), when "some Orestes" is first mentioned, to 414. One may remember that (1) the name Orestes means "mountaineer," i.e. savage, (2) the hero Orestes was mad, (3) it was bad luck to meet any hero.

PATROCLIDES: unknown.

PEISIAS: Little is known of him. In ll. 1292 ff. he is a "lame shop-keeper" and is called "partridge"; that cunning bird which leads people away from its nest by pretending to be lame. His son apparently had some project of granting an amnesty to persons condemned for treason—a policy which Aristophanes himself favoured later in the *Frogs* (686 ff.)

PHARNAKES: the Persian; Satrap of the Hellespontine region, a powerful enemy of Athens.

PHILEMON: a politician otherwise unknown.

PHILIPPUS: disciple of the famous Sicilian orator and sophist, Gorgias. In the *Wasps* (421) we hear that he was "stung" by those insects in some case.

PHILOCLES: a tragic poet, nephew of Aeschylus. He wrote a tetralogy, *Pandionis*, of which one play was *Tereus*. His style was "harsh," as that of Sophocles was "sweet" (*Wasps*, 462). "A poet's work must come from his nature; Theognis, being cold, writes cold stuff; Philocles, being ugly, ugly stuff" (*Thesm.*, 168). Nevertheless, Sophocles' masterpiece, the *Oedipus Rex*, was defeated by an unknown play of his.

PHILOCRATES: a poulterer and bird-seller, only known from this play.

PHRYNICHUS: the tragedian, was an older contemporary of Aeschylus; His *Phoenissae*, like the *Persae* of Aeschylus, celebrated the Battle of Salamis. His lyrics were loved by the older Athenians as being filled with "wild honey and the East and loveliness." (*Wasps*, l. 220.) Aristophanes mentions two other men of the name, a comic poet whose *Solitary*, produced the same year as *The Birds*, won the third prize; and an oligarchic politician.

PISANDER: A fat and greedy demagogue, like Cleonymus; often called an ass or connected with asses;

perhaps he kept a livery-stable for them. In the *Babylonians* he is a stirrer up of war. Lysias adds: "because war is a convenient time for stealing in." In the *Peace* (395), Pisander's "crests and eyebrows" make decent people sick. Yet Eupolis says that wherever he wandered he was still the greatest coward in the army, and Xenophon that he "could not look a spear in the face" (*Conv.* 2, 14). He outbid Cleonymus in stimulating the popular terror about the Hermae; joined the Four Hundred; fled to the Spartans. His "spirit," or courage, had been lost, and he could not recover it. (1556 ff.)

PRODICUS: one of the most famous of the Sophists. His fable on "The Choice of Heracles"—between the broad downward path and the narrow upward— is proverbial. He is mentioned in l. 692, where I have put "the astronomers."

PROXENIDES: a boaster, dismissed as so much "smoke" or "hot air" in *Wasps*, l. 324. Otherwise unknown.

SAKAS: a name for Scythians, cf. words like "Dago," or "Hunkey." In l. 31 there is evidently a hit at some particular person.

SIMONIDES: the lyric poet, contemporary with Pindar. Many fragments of his work are extant; his epitaph on those who died at Thermopylae is specially famous.

SKELIAS: only known through his son Aristocrates. See above.

SPINTHARUS: called "a Phrygian"; otherwise unknown.

SPORGILUS: a barber of the time, his shop no doubt a great meeting-place. Plato (Comicus) refers in a tragic parody to "The shaving shop Of Sporgilus, abode detestable."

SYRACOSIUS: author of a resolution passed by the Assembly in 415 B.C. prohibiting personal attacks in Comedy, hence not popular with the comic poets. Here he is a "jay"; in Eupolis he is a "barking dog." (The name, meaning "Syracusan," is like "Opuntius" or like "Amerikanos" in modern Greece.)

TELEAS: He was Secretary to the Committee of Treasurers in charge of the Treasure of the Parthenon. He has a bad name in comedy; an irresponsible "bird-man" (l. 168), a glutton (*Peace*, l. 1008) and one of the "large apes" like Exekestides. (Phrynichus fr. 20).

THEOGENES: the boaster (ll. 822, 1127), though "mere hot air" (Eupolis) and a "goose-fox" (l. 1295), was quite an important person. He went with Cleon to Pylos in 425, was a signatory of the peace in 421, was on an embassy to the Great King in 408, and became one of the Thirty Tyrants in 404.

TIMON: the misanthrope, known to us by Shakespeare's play and Lucian's dialogue, was a real man, son of Echecrates, of the deme Collytus. There are many anecdotes about him.

TRIBALLI: a particularly savage and independent Thracian tribe, whose territory was probably about the plain of Kossovo in Serbia.

XANTHIAS: like Manes, a regular slave-name. It may be derived from the river Xanthos in Lydia, or from the adjective meaning "auburn."

DATE DUE	